HOUSING ISSUES, LAWS AND PROGRAMS

HOUSING FINANCE REFORM IN AMERICA

HOUSING ISSUES, LAWS AND PROGRAMS

Additional books in this series can be found on Nova's website under the Series tab.

Additional E-books in this series can be found on Nova's website under the E-books tab.

AMERICAN POLITICAL, ECONOMIC, AND SECURITY ISSUES

Additional books in this series can be found on Nova's website under the Series tab.

Additional E-books in this series can be found on Nova's website under the E-books tab.

HOUSING ISSUES, LAWS AND PROGRAMS

HOUSING FINANCE REFORM IN AMERICA

BENJAMIN W. VIRTANEN
AND
ELIAS A. LAINE
EDITORS

Nova Science Publishers, Inc.
New York

For permission to use material from this book please contact us:
Telephone 631-231-7269; Fax 631-231-8175
Web Site: http://www.novapublishers.com

Library of Congress Cataloging-in-Publication Data

Housing finance reform in America / editors, Benjamin W. Virtanen and Elias A. Laine.
p. cm.
Includes index.
ISBN 978-1-61324-350-3 (softcover)
1. Housing--Finance--Government policy--United States. 2. Federal National Mortgage Association. 3. Freddie Mac (Firm) I. Virtanen, Benjamin W. II. Laine, Elias A. III. Title.
HD7293.Z9H679 2011
332.7'220973--dc22

2011011439

Published by Nova Science Publishers, Inc. † New York

CONTENTS

PREFACE

This book examines the Administration's plan to reform America's housing finance market to better serve families and function more safely in a world that has changed dramatically since its original pillars were put in place nearly eighty years ago. Americans should have choices in housing that make sense for them and for their families. This means rental options near good schools and good jobs, as well as access to credit for those Americans who want to own their own home, which has helped millions of middle class families build wealth and achieve the American Dream. Going forward, the government's primary role should be limited to robust oversight and consumer protection, targeted assistance for low-and moderate-income homeowners and renters, and carefully designed support for market stability and crisis response.

Chapter 1- This paper lays out the Administration's plan to reform America's housing finance market to better serve families and function more safely in a world that has changed dramatically since its original pillars were put in place nearly eighty years ago.

Our plan champions the belief that Americans should have choices in housing that make sense for them and for their families. This means rental options near good schools and good jobs. It means access to credit for those Americans who want to own their own home, which has helped millions of middle class families build wealth and achieve the American Dream. And it means a helping hand for lower-income Americans, who are burdened by the strain of high housing costs.

Chapter 2- The conservatorship of Fannie Mae and Freddie Mac raises questions about the impact of these government-sponsored enterprises (GSEs) on the housing and finance markets and their ability to return to financial viability. To date, the federal government has purchased more than $148 billion in stock in the two companies, with pending requests from Fannie Mae to purchase an additional $2.5 billion and from Freddie Mac for $100 million. Once these transactions are completed, the Treasury will hold $152.8 billion in senior preferred stock. Both companies are required under terms of the federal support to pay the government dividends of more than $15 billion annually (10% of the support). Housing, mortgage, and even general financial markets remain in an unprecedented situation.

Chapter 3- This report analyzes some options that Congress might wish to consider for the future of Fannie Mae and Freddie Mac, which are federally chartered, stockholder-owned corporations known as government-sponsored enterprises or GSEs.

As GSEs, Fannie Mae and Freddie Mac have special privileges and obligations. Their charters give them a close relationship to the federal government that was widely (but not universally) viewed as an implicit federal guarantee of their bonds and mortgage-backed securities (MBS). The Housing and Economic Recovery Act of 2008 (HERA, P.L. 110-289) authorizes the Secretary of the Treasury to purchase unlimited amounts of obligations and other securities from the GSEs.

Housing Finance Reform in America
Editors: B. W. Virtanen, E. A. Laine
ISBN: 978-1-61324-350-3

Chapter 1

REFORMING AMERICA'S HOUSING FINANCE MARKET: A REPORT TO CONGRESS*

U.S. Department of Housing and Urban Development

INTRODUCTION

This paper lays out the Administration's plan to reform America's housing finance market to better serve families and function more safely in a world that has changed dramatically since its original pillars were put in place nearly eighty years ago.

Our plan champions the belief that Americans should have choices in housing that make sense for them and for their families. This means rental options near good schools and good jobs. It means access to credit for those Americans who want to own their own home, which has helped millions of middle class families build wealth and achieve the American Dream. And it means a helping hand for lower-income Americans, who are burdened by the strain of high housing costs.

But our plan also dramatically transforms the role of government in the housing market. In the past, the government's financial and tax policies encouraged housing purchases and real estate investment over other sectors of our economy, and ultimately left taxpayers responsible for much of the risk incurred by a poorly supervised housing finance market.

---

* This is an edited, reformatted and augmented version of the U.S. Department of Housing and Urban Development publication, dated February 2011.

Going forward, the government's primary role should be limited to robust oversight and consumer protection, targeted assistance for low- and moderate-income homeowners and renters, and carefully designed support for market stability and crisis response. Our plan helps ensure that our nation's economic health will not be jeopardized again by the fundamental flaws in the housing market that existed before the financial crisis. At the same time, this plan recognizes the fragile state of our housing market and is designed to ensure that reforms are implemented at a stable and measured pace to support economic recovery over the next several years.

Under our plan, private markets – subject to strong oversight and standards for consumer and investor protection – will be the primary source of mortgage credit and bear the burden for losses. Banks and other financial institutions will be required to hold more capital to withstand future recessions or significant declines in home prices, and adhere to more conservative underwriting standards that require homeowners to hold more equity in their homes. Securitization, alongside credit from the banking system, should continue to play a major role in housing finance subject to greater risk retention, disclosure, and other key reforms. Our plan is also designed to eliminate unfair capital, oversight, and accounting advantages and promote a level playing field for all participants in the housing market.

The Administration will work with the Federal Housing Finance Agency ("FHFA") to develop a plan to responsibly reduce the role of the Federal National Mortgage Association ("Fannie Mae") and the Federal Home Loan Mortgage Corporation ("Freddie Mac") in the mortgage market and, ultimately, wind down both institutions. We recommend FHFA employ a number of policy levers – including increased guarantee fee pricing, increased down payment requirements, and other measures – to bring private capital back into the mortgage market and reduce taxpayer risk. As the market improves and Fannie Mae and Freddie Mac are wound down, it should be clear that the government is committed to ensuring that Fannie Mae and Freddie Mac have sufficient capital to perform under any guarantees issued now or in the future and the ability to meet any of their debt obligations. We believe that under our current Preferred Stock Purchase Agreements (PSPAs), there is sufficient funding to ensure the orderly and deliberate wind down of Fannie Mae and Freddie Mac, as described in our plan.

Successful reform will require more than just winding down Fannie Mae and Freddie Mac and reducing other government support to the housing market. In addition to fully implementing the reforms in the Dodd-Frank Wall Street Reform and Consumer Protection Act ("Dodd-Frank Act") (Pub. L.

111-203), the Administration will mobilize all tools available to address the nation's broken system of mortgage servicing and foreclosure processing. Taken together, these steps will help restore trust in the underlying foundation of the mortgage market so borrowers, lenders, and investors have the confidence to purchase a home, issue a loan, or make an investment.

The government must also help ensure that all Americans have access to quality housing that they can afford. This does not mean our goal is for all Americans to be homeowners. We should continue to provide targeted and effective support to families with the financial capacity and desire to own a home, but who are underserved by the private market, as well as a range of options for Americans who rent their homes.

Finally, our plan presents several proposals for structuring the government's long-term role in a housing finance system in which the private sector is the dominant provider of mortgage credit. We evaluate these proposals according to their effects on four key criteria: access to mortgage credit; incentives for investment in the housing sector; taxpayer protection; and financial and economic stability. We ask Congress to work with us to determine the right balance of priorities for a new, predominantly private housing finance market as soon as possible.

Reform will not come overnight. Some reforms can take place immediately, like improvements to consumer protection and government oversight, while others will be implemented more gradually as the housing market heals.

We welcome the opportunity to work with Congress, independent regulators and agencies, and a wide range of stakeholders and partners to meet the goals laid out in the pages below.

HOUSING FINANCE FROM THE GREAT DEPRESSION TO THE GREAT RECESSION

Nearly eighty years ago, in the midst of the Great Depression, the federal government began implementing sweeping reforms to the American financial system. These reforms – deposit insurance, limits on the risks banks can take, better transparency and investor protections in securities markets, a stronger Federal Reserve – helped build a financial system that provided a solid foundation for America's unprecedented prosperity.

Improving how housing was financed was an important part of these broader Depression-era reforms. In the 1930s, following severe mortgage market disruptions, widespread foreclosures, and sinking homeownership rates, the government created the Federal Housing Administration ("FHA"), Fannie Mae, the Federal Home Loan Banks ("FHLBs") and, several decades later, Freddie Mac to help promote secure and sustainable homeownership for future generations of Americans.

Fannie Mae and Freddie Mac held true to their original mission for many years. They established appropriate benchmarks for conforming loans that drove improved standards within the broader mortgage industry. They helped reduce rates for borrowers by bringing transparency and standardization to the housing finance market. They played a central role in the development of securitization of conventional mortgages, which expanded access to homeownership for responsible borrowers, providing a much-needed link between places with established banking services and growing parts of the country without local funding sources for mortgages. For decades, borrowers, lenders, and investors benefited from the deep, liquid markets these institutions helped establish. This same marketplace gave American families access to simple, straightforward products, protecting them from sudden financial shocks and helping them build savings in their homes.

But in the years leading up to the recent financial crisis, trillions of dollars worth of financial decisions were made across the U.S. economy and around the world on the faulty expectation that national house prices would only rise. Twenty years of economic stability had desensitized every player in the housing market to the possibility that home prices could fall.

Indeed, despite occasional regional price declines, national home values in America had not declined on a consistent basis since the Depression. But in the years leading up to the recent crisis, a robust expansion in credit, fueled by processes and financial instruments designed to shift risk away from originators, combined with other factors, fed a rising demand for housing that lifted prices well above sustainable values. Average home values in many parts of the country skyrocketed. Mortgages became tools for speculative, short-term investments and a means to access easy cash. Lulled into a false sense of an ever-rising real estate market, some homebuyers took on more debt than they could afford to purchase homes beyond their means, and existing homeowners used their homes like ATM machines by converting home equity to cash.

By mid-2006, however, housing prices across a broad range of markets began to turn, eventually declining consistently for the first time since the

1930s. Almost no one in the housing finance market was prepared. Homeowners, investors, and financial institutions – including Fannie Mae and Freddie Mac – did not have enough capital supporting their investments to absorb the resulting losses. In 2008, credit markets froze. Our nation's financial system – which had outgrown and outmaneuvered a regulatory framework largely designed in the 1930s – was driven to the brink of collapse. Millions of Americans lost their jobs, families lost their homes, and small businesses shut down. Fannie Mae and Freddie Mac experienced catastrophic losses and were placed into conservatorship, where they remain today.

Fundamental Flaws in the Housing Finance Market

No single cause can fully explain the crisis. Misbehavior, misjudgments, and missed opportunities – on Wall Street, on Main Street, and in Washington – all came together to push the economy to the brink of collapse. Several fundamental flaws in our housing finance system contributed to the crisis and must be corrected to protect American families from the instabilities and excesses that helped bring us to a crisis point.

- *Poor consumer protections allowed risky, low-quality mortgage products and predatory lending to proliferate:* Unregulated brokers and originators promoted complex mortgage products that "reset" to sharply higher rates after a few years, or required no income documentation or down payment. Some allowed borrowers to defer principal and interest payments, increasing their indebtedness over time. Often, brokers and originators had incentives to steer borrowers into these higher-cost loans, even if they qualified for more affordable options. Some speculators knowingly took on loans they could not afford, betting that future housing price increases would bail them out. Millions of borrowers who purchased these products proved unable to make required payments, resulting in widespread defaults and foreclosures once housing prices started to fall.
- *An inadequate and outdated regulatory regime failed to keep the system in check:* Regulatory boundaries largely unchanged from the 1930s allowed large parts of the financial system that were deeply involved in housing finance to operate with virtually no oversight. To be sure, there were some problems that arose from violations of the law. In many cases, however, weak and fragmented regulation and

enforcement also allowed lenders to "shop" for weaker oversight and drove deteriorating standards in lending practices. Securitizers and investors could essentially opt-out of the parts of the system with heavier regulation and use whatever underwriting practices they saw fit. Other actors in the system were allowed to avoid consistent regulation and choose favorable jurisdictions.

- *A complex securitization chain lacked transparency, standardization, and accountability:* The market increasingly relied on an opaque and complex securitization chain – comprised of mortgage brokers, originators, securitizers, ratings agencies, and investors – to provide the money that helped fuel the rapid rise in home prices. Brokers and originators could profit from selling poorly underwritten mortgages to securitizers without regard to those loans' future performance. Ratings agencies and investors failed to recognize that the deterioration in underwriting standards had undermined the quality of complex mortgage-backed securities. An overall lack of transparency and clear rules made it difficult for regulators and investors to track and recognize risk as it moved through the securitization chain.
- *Inadequate capital in the system left financial institutions unprepared to absorb losses.* Systemically-significant financial institutions were not required to hold adequate capital against the true mortgage risk on their balance sheets because these institutions were allowed to hold less capital against securities backed by mortgages than if they kept the same mortgages themselves. When home prices started to fall and these institutions experienced substantial losses, they had inadequate capital to weather the storm, putting the health of the entire financial system and broader economy at risk.
- The servicing industry was ill-equipped to serve the needs of borrowers, lenders, and investors once housing prices fell. The servicing industry, which processes borrower payments and forwards the proceeds to investors who own the pool of mortgages, was unprepared and poorly structured to address the higher levels of default and foreclosure that occurred after the housing market collapse. Servicing contracts did a poor job defining the obligations of servicers to minimize losses on defaulting loans. Servicers' flat fee compensation structure also failed to provide appropriate incentives for servicers to invest the time, effort, and resources necessary to prevent foreclosure, even when doing so would have been in both the homeowner and mortgage investors' interests.

The Failure of Fannie Mae and Freddie Mac

Initially, Fannie Mae and Freddie Mac were largely on the sidelines while private markets generated increasingly risky mortgages. Between 2001 and 2005, private-label securitizations of Alt-A and subprime mortgages grew fivefold, yet Fannie Mae and Freddie Mac continued to primarily guarantee fully documented, high-quality mortgages.

But as their combined market share declined – from nearly 70 percent of new originations in 2003 to 40 percent in 2006 – Fannie Mae and Freddie Mac pursued riskier business to raise their market share and increase profits. Not only did they expand their guarantees to new and riskier products, but they also increased their holdings of some of these riskier mortgages on their own balance sheets.

Fannie Mae and Freddie Mac strayed farthest from their core business in 2006 and 2007 – the very moment the housing market was extending credit to the riskiest borrowers and home prices were peaking. When home prices began to fall and adjustable-rate mortgages with low teaser rates reset to higher rates, the Alt-A mortgages that Fannie Mae and Freddie Mac had accumulated started to default at alarming rates.

By 2008, mortgages across the product spectrum, including high-credit, well-documented prime mortgages, were defaulting at historically high rates. Fannie Mae and Freddie Mac's losses had become far too substantial for their thin capital buffers to absorb, and it became clear they would be unable to fully honor their debts and guarantees. In September of 2008, in consultation with the Bush Administration, FHFA placed Fannie Mae and Freddie Mac in conservatorship under the authority provided by the Housing and Economic Recovery Act of 2008 ("HERA") (Pub. L. 110-289), which Congress had passed to support the housing market two months earlier. The Treasury Department agreed to exercise its authority under HERA to provide financial support – to date, over $130 billion – so both Fannie Mae and Freddie Mac could honor their debt and guarantees. These measures, though unfortunate, were necessary to prevent a more severe disruption in the mortgage market and broader economy.

Fannie Mae and Freddie Mac's structural design flaws, combined with failures in management, were the primary cause of their collapse. Although some have suggested affordability goals played a major role, the mistakes that led to the failure of Fannie Mae and Freddie Mac – poor underwriting standards, under pricing risk, and insufficient capital with inadequate regulatory or investor oversight – closely mirrored mistakes in the private-label securities (PLS) market where affordability goals were not a factor. In fact, delinquency rates on many PLS securities and other loans held by banks and other private market institutions were far higher than on the loans held by Fannie Mae and Freddie Mac, including loans qualifying for the affordability goals. While Fannie Mae and Freddie Mac's affordability goals were poorly designed and did not effectively serve their purposes (as detailed below), fundamental structural flaws and poor decision-making are the principal reasons these institutions failed.

- *Fannie Mae and Freddie Mac's profit-maximizing structure undermined their public mission.* Fannie Mae and Freddie Mac's congressional charters require them to promote market stability and access to mortgage credit. But their private shareholder structure, coupled with a weak oversight regime, encouraged management to take on excessive risk in order to retain market share and maximize profits, jeopardizing their ability to support the mortgage market and leaving taxpayers to bear major losses. Their pursuit of profit leading up to the financial crisis caused them to fail when their broader public mandate to support the market was needed most.
- *Fannie Mae and Freddie Mac's perceived government backing conferred unfair advantages.* Fannie Mae and Freddie Mac benefited from preferential tax treatment, far lower capital requirements, and a widely perceived government guarantee – the commonly held assumption that large losses would be backstopped by the taxpayer. These advantages gave them substantial pricing power that helped them dominate segments of the market in which they participated, build up large investment portfolios at a cost far lower than their competitors, and take on irresponsible risks through their guarantee business that ultimately resulted in their failure.
- *Fannie Mae and Freddie Mac's capital standards were unfair and inadequate.* Fannie Mae and Freddie Mac were required to hold far less capital than other regulated private institutions. Since they did not have to maintain higher levels of capital, they could set the fee that they charged to guarantee mortgage-backed securities at artificially low levels. It also left them with an inadequate cushion to absorb losses once the housing crisis hit.
- *Fannie Mae and Freddie Mac's regulator was structurally weak and ineffective.* The Office of Federal Housing Enterprise Oversight ("OFHEO"), Fannie Mae and Freddie Mac's previous regulator, did

> not have adequate enforcement mechanisms or authority to set capital standards to constrain risky behavior. Over the years, Fannie Mae and Freddie Mac's aggressive lobbying efforts had successfully defeated efforts to bring them under closer supervision.

The financial crisis also exacerbated fundamental flaws in the FHLBs, which help mostly insured depository institutions access liquidity and capital to compete in an increasingly competitive marketplace. Prior to the crisis, the FHLBs suffered from inadequate regulatory oversight, and were allowed to build large investment portfolios that subjected them to excess risk, while providing concentrated funding to banks engaging in unsound business practices. Today, eight of the twelve banks are under regulatory orders with respect to their capital or have voluntarily suspended dividends or the repurchase of excess stock.

Because each of the twelve FHLBs is also liable for the losses of other FHLBs, additional losses could adversely affect the entire FHLB system, damaging the mortgage finance market and potentially constraining access to capital for financial institutions. Reforms to the FHLB system are necessary to restore its important primary role of providing a stable source of mortgage credit for financial institutions of all sizes.

The Current State of the Housing Market

Since taking office in January 2009, the Obama Administration has acted to help stabilize the housing market and provide critical support for struggling homeowners. The Administration worked with Congress to put in place expanded tax credits for first-time homebuyers, additional support for state and local housing agencies, neighborhood stabilization and community development programs, mortgage modification and refinancing initiatives, housing counseling programs, expanded support for mortgage credit through FHA, and strengthened consumer protections. The Administration has also provided ongoing financial support for Fannie Mae and Freddie Mac through the PSPAs following the Bush Administration's decision to put that support in place and FHFA's decision to place them into conservatorship.

These policies helped avert a deeper economic collapse and a more severe housing crisis. However, the housing market remains fragile and will take years to fully recover. An elevated unemployment rate, lower household wealth, and higher credit standards are constraining demand for housing. Sales of new and existing homes are well below their recent peaks. At the same time, the large inventory of unsold homes, including a backlog of foreclosed homes that have yet to appear on the market, will take an extended period to work through the system. As a result of both supply and demand factors, housing construction is at historically low levels, and home prices remain weak.

TOWARDS A NEW SYSTEM OF HOUSING FINANCE

The Obama Administration has already begun the critical process of reforming our nation's housing finance market. The Dodd-Frank Act, enacted in July 2010, provides vital protections for consumers and investors that will help end abusive practices in the mortgage market and improve the stability of the overall housing finance system.

Since Fannie Mae and Freddie Mac were placed into conservatorship, the FHFA has monitored their business operations closely and strengthened underwriting standards, reducing risk to the American taxpayers. Since 2008, FICO scores and loan-to-value ratios – both key measures of how likely a borrower will be to make mortgage payments – are meaningfully better on new mortgages. Fannie Mae and Freddie Mac have also increased their guarantee fees and adjusted their pricing to better reflect risk. The FHA has also implemented important changes and reforms over the last two years, including strengthening underwriting standards, improving processes and operations, and raising premiums to improve its financial condition.

But these measures are only first steps. We must move forward with additional reforms to better protect taxpayers and improve the long-term health of the housing market.

The Obama Administration's reform plan is designed to:

1) Pave the way for a robust private mortgage market by reducing government support for housing finance and winding down Fannie Mae and Freddie Mac on a responsible timeline.
2) Address fundamental flaws in the mortgage market to protect borrowers, help ensure transparency for investors, and increase the role of private capital.
3) Target the government's vital support for affordable housing in a more effective and transparent manner.

Any responsible reform effort that addresses the flaws in the pre-crisis housing market will make credit less easily available than before the crisis. Any such changes should occur at a measured pace that allows borrowers to adjust to the new market, that preserves widespread access to affordable mortgages for creditworthy borrowers, including lower-income Americans, and that supports, rather than threatens, the nation's economic recovery.

I. Paving the Way for a Robust Private Mortgage Market

In the wake of the financial crisis, private capital has not sufficiently returned to the mortgage market, leaving Fannie Mae, Freddie Mac, FHA, and the Government National Mortgage Association ("Ginnie Mae") to insure or guarantee more than nine out of every ten new mortgages.

Under normal market conditions, the essential components of housing finance – buying houses, lending money, determining how best to invest capital, and bearing credit risk – are fundamentally private sector activities. Although the government still has an important role to play in housing finance, private markets – subject to strong oversight and standards for consumer and investor protection – should be the primary source of mortgage credit and bear the burden for losses. The Obama Administration, in consultation with FHFA and Congress, will work to restrict the areas of mortgage finance in which Fannie Mae, Freddie Mac, and the FHLBs operate, so that overall government support is substantially reduced.

Our commitment to ensuring Fannie Mae and Freddie Mac have sufficient capital to honor any guarantees issued now or in the future and meet any of their debt obligations remains unchanged. Ensuring these institutions have the financial capacity to meet their obligations is essential to continued stability, and the Administration will not waver from its commitment. Given Fannie Mae and Freddie Mac's current role in the mortgage market, we must proceed carefully with reform to ensure government support is withdrawn at a pace that does not undermine economic recovery. We believe that under the PSPAs, there is sufficient funding to ensure the orderly and deliberate wind down of Fannie Mae and Freddie Mac, as described in our plan.

Winding Down Fannie Mae and Freddie Mac on a Responsible Timeline

The Administration will work with FHFA to determine the best way to responsibly reduce Fannie Mae and Freddie Mac's role in the market and ultimately wind down both institutions, creating the conditions for private capital to play the predominant role in housing finance. These efforts must be undertaken at a deliberate pace, which takes into account the impact that these changes will have on borrowers and the housing market.

- *Increasing guarantee fees to bring in more private capital.* We support ending the unfair capital advantages that Fannie Mae and Freddie Mac previously enjoyed and recommend FHFA require that they price their guarantees as if they were held to the same capital standards as private banks or financial institutions. This will mean that the price of the guarantee offered by Fannie Mae and Freddie Mac explicitly reflects its risk, and will help the private market compete on a level playing field, reducing Fannie Mae and Freddie Mac's market share over time. Although the pace of these price changes will depend significantly on market conditions, such changes should be phased in over the next several years.
- *Increasing private capital ahead of Fannie Mae and Freddie Mac guarantees.* In addition to increasing guarantee pricing, we will encourage Fannie Mae and Freddie Mac to pursue additional credit-loss protection from private insurers and other capital providers. We also support increasing the level of private capital ahead of Fannie Mae and Freddie Mac's guarantees by requiring larger down payments by borrowers. Going forward, we support gradually increasing the level of required down payment so that any mortgages insured by Fannie Mae or Freddie Mac eventually have at least a ten percent down payment.
- *Reducing conforming loan limits.* The conforming loan limit is the maximum size of a loan that Fannie Mae and Freddie Mac are

allowed to guarantee. In order to further scale back the enterprises' share of the mortgage market, the Administration recommends that Congress allow the temporary increase in limits that was approved in 2008 to expire as scheduled on October 1, 2011 and revert to the limits established under HERA. We will work with Congress to determine appropriate conforming loan limits in the future, taking into account cost-of-living differences across the country. As a result of these reforms, larger loans for more expensive homes will once again be funded only through the private market.

- *Winding down Fannie Mae and Freddie Mac's investment portfolio.* Fannie Mae and Freddie Mac were allowed to behave like government-backed hedge funds, managing large investment portfolios for the profit of their shareholders with the risk ultimately falling largely on taxpayers. The PSPAs require a reduction in this risk-taking by winding down their investment portfolios at an annual pace of no less than 10 percent.

Implementing a wind down of Fannie Mae and Freddie Mac's future participation in the housing market requires recognition of both the fragile state of that market today and the private sector's need for clarity about the speed with which that transition will take place. As the market begins to heal and private investors return, we will seek opportunities, wherever possible, to accelerate Fannie Mae and Freddie Mac's withdrawal.

Returning FHA to Its Traditional Role as Targeted Lender of Affordable Mortgages

In addition to winding down Fannie Mae and Freddie Mac, FHA should return to its pre-crisis role as a targeted provider of mortgage credit access for low- and moderate-income Americans and first-time homebuyers. (Today, FHA's market share is nearly 30 percent, compared to its historic role of between 10-15 percent.) As Fannie Mae and Freddie Mac's presence in the market shrinks, the Administration will coordinate program changes at FHA to ensure that the private market – not FHA – picks up that new market share.

To accomplish this objective, we recommend decreasing the maximum loan size that can qualify for FHA insurance – first by allowing the present increase in those limits to expire as scheduled on October 1, 2011, and then by reviewing whether those limits should be further decreased moving forward. As we begin to pursue increased pricing for guarantees at Fannie Mae and Freddie Mac, we will also increase the price of FHA mortgage insurance. We have already acted on this front, raising premiums two times since the beginning of this Administration. And we will put in place another 25 basis point increase in the annual mortgage insurance premium that is detailed in the President's 2012 Budget. This will continue the ongoing effort to strengthen the capital reserve account of FHA, and put it in a better position to gradually shrink its market share. Going forward we will coordinate reforms of Fannie Mae and Freddie Mac with changes at FHA to help ensure the private market, not FHA, fills the market opportunities created by reform.

Ensuring FHLB Support for Small- and Medium-Sized Financial Institutions

The Administration believes the FHLBs have played a vital role in our housing finance system by helping smaller financial institutions effectively access liquidity to compete in an increasingly competitive marketplace. But these institutions also developed significant weaknesses as the housing market evolved that should be addressed as part of housing finance reform. HERA has already placed the FHLBs under stricter regulatory oversight, but further reform is required. We will also work with Congress to consider additional means of advance funding for mortgage credit, including potentially the development of a covered bond market.

- *Focusing on small- and medium-sized financial institutions*. The Administration supports allowing each financial institution to be an active member in only a single FHLB Bank. We also support limiting the level of advances, which would only have an impact on large financial institutions that can access capital markets already.
- *Reducing portfolio investments.* Similar to Fannie Mae and Freddie Mac, several of the FHLBs were allowed to build up large investment portfolios. These portfolios should be reduced and their composition altered to better serve the FHLB's mission of providing liquidity and access to capital for insured depository institutions. We support FHFA's efforts to address this issue, and we will work with Congress to provide clarity to the FHLB's investment authority.

Improving Coordination among Existing Government Housing Finance Programs

In addition to changing the level of government support for the housing market, we also must reform the way government support is delivered. The Department of Housing and Urban Development, the Department of

Agriculture, and the Department of Veterans Affairs will set up a task force to explore ways in which their housing finance programs can be better coordinated, or even consolidated, to serve the public more effectively. Though they serve different targeted groups of Americans, their programs and borrowers will benefit from greater coordination of systems, information, and market standards.

II. Restoring Trust and Integrity in the Broader Housing Market

Addressing Fannie Mae, Freddie Mac, FHA, and the FHLBs alone will not give rise to a housing finance market that meets the needs of families, lenders, and investors. Nor will it guarantee that private markets can effectively play a more dominant role in the mortgage market. Fundamental flaws occurred at almost every link in the housing finance chain.

The Administration supports the vigorous implementation of reforms to help address pre-crisis flaws and rebuild trust and integrity in the mortgage market. Taken together, these reforms will improve consumer protection, support the creation of safe, high-quality mortgage products with strong underwriting standards, restore the integrity of the securitization market, restructure the servicing industry, and establish clear and consolidated regulatory oversight.

The Dodd-Frank Act laid the groundwork for many of these reforms. We will implement its provisions in a thoughtful manner to protect borrowers and promote stability across the housing finance markets. Together, these reforms will form the foundation of a market in which borrowers, lenders, investors – along with the broader economy – will all be better off.

Empowering Consumers to Avoid Unfair Practices and Make Fully Informed Decisions

The Administration is committed to full implementation of the Dodd-Frank Act's consumer protection provisions, including the following:

- *Curbing abusive practices.* Under rules to be developed by the Bureau of Consumer Financial Protection ("CFPB"), which was created by the Dodd-Frank Act, lenders will be prohibited from originating high-cost loans with certain abusive features, and mortgage brokers and other originators will be prohibited from accepting financial rewards for steering borrowers into more expensive products than those for which they are qualified.

- *Promoting choice and clarity.* The CFPB also will have the authority to set clear, consistent rules that allow financial services providers to compete on a level playing field and let consumers clearly see the costs and features of consumer financial products and services. The CFPB will take steps to improve and simplify the required disclosures for mortgage loan transactions to promote fairness, transparency, and competition in the mortgage market.
- *Stronger underwriting standards, including requiring lenders to verify ability to pay.* Under rules to be prescribed by the CFPB, lenders will be required to make a reasonable and good-faith determination that all borrowers have a reasonable ability to repay their mortgage, including by verifying a borrower's income.

Increasing Transparency, Standardization, and Accountability in the Securitization Chain

The Administration believes the securitization market should continue to play a key role in housing finance. That market, however, requires meaningful reform so private investors can confidently participate in the housing market and provide an alternative funding source for mortgages outside of the traditional banking system and government-supported institutions.

- *Requiring originators and securitizers to retain risk.* The Administration is working with federal regulators to set rules requiring securitizers or originators to retain five percent of a security's credit risk when sold to investors. Combined with an exemption for mortgages that meet high underwriting standards (Qualified Residential Mortgages, or "QRM"), this requirement will improve alignment of interests between mortgage originators, securitizers, and investors. Rules will be finalized in 2011 and become effective in 2012.
- *Improving access to information among all market participants.* The SEC will implement Dodd-Frank Act provisions that set stricter disclosure and reporting requirements so that regulators and investors can more easily understand the underlying collateral and risks of securities.
- *Strengthen transparency and disclosure in credit ratings agencies' analysis.* The Securities and Exchange Commission ("SEC") will

establish an Office of Credit Ratings. This new office will have dedicated compliance resources with the ability to improve disclosure for ratings methodologies, set new requirements to prohibit conflicts of interest, and authorize the SEC to deregister ratings agencies that perform poorly.

Increasing Capital Standards to Improve the Safety and Stability of the Financial System

The Basel III Capital Accords will substantially increase the overall amount of capital that banks are required to hold on their balance sheets. These measures will improve the ability of banks to withstand future downturns, declines in home prices, and other sudden economic shocks, which will help improve the safety and stability of the financial system and broader economy. These new standards will also require banks to hold larger capital buffers against higher-risk mortgages that have a greater risk of default, providing strong incentives to originate higher-quality mortgages.

Strengthening Regulatory Oversight

The Dodd-Frank Act provides a comprehensive approach to monitor and constrain excessive risk in the financial system, and to strengthen the transparency and resilience of financial markets.

- *Closing regulatory gaps.* The newly created Financial Stability Oversight Council ("FSOC") has the authority to require consolidated supervision of any financial firm – regardless of legal form – whose failure could pose a threat to financial stability. The Act also eliminates regulatory arbitrage for nationally chartered depository institutions by eliminating the Office of Thrift Supervision and moving that authority into the Office of the Comptroller of the Currency.
- *Monitoring systemic risk.* The Dodd-Frank Act creates accountability in the FSOC for taking a comprehensive approach to monitoring the nation's financial system. The FSOC is charged with identifying threats to the financial stability of the United States, promoting market discipline, and responding to emerging risks to the stability of the United States financial system, including mortgage markets.

Improving Mortgage Servicing and Foreclosure Processing

The Administration supports several immediate and near-term reforms to correct problems in mortgage servicing and foreclosure processing and help prevent their recurrence.

- *Establishing national standards for mortgage servicing.* Servicers should manage each loan that they service promptly and appropriately. The Administration supports national servicing standards that better align incentives and provide clarity and consistency to borrowers and investors regarding their treatment by servicers, especially in the event of delinquency.
- *Reforming servicing compensation to align industry incentives.* The Administration is working with FHFA, in coordination with HUD, to explore alternative servicing compensation structures to align industry incentives. Currently, servicers collect a flat fee that does not adjust to reflect the amount of work they are required to perform, resulting in overpayment for servicing current loans and underpayment for servicing delinquent loans. A compensation structure that corrects for the current structure's shortcomings could help ensure servicers are appropriately incentivized to invest the time and effort to work with troubled borrowers to avoid default or foreclosure.
- *Improving treatment of lien priority.* We should reduce conflicts of interests between holders of first and second mortgages and improve transparency for lenders and borrowers regarding the total debt secured by a given piece of property. Mortgage documents should require disclosure of second liens. In addition, mortgage documents should define the process for modifying a second lien in the event that the first lien becomes delinquent. This will prevent a second lien from standing in the way of a first lien modification and help prevent avoidable foreclosures. Finally, we should consider options for allowing primary mortgage holders to restrict, in certain circumstances, additional debt secured by the same property.

III. A System with Transparent and Targeted Support for Access and Affordability

The Administration believes that we must continue to take the necessary steps to ensure that Americans have access to an adequate range of affordable housing options. This does not mean all Americans should become homeowners. Instead, we should make sure that all Americans who have the credit history, financial capacity, and desire to own a home have the opportunity to take that step. At the same time, we should ensure that there are a range of affordable options for the 100 million Americans who rent, whether they do so by choice or necessity.

In the past, broader government efforts to support affordability through Fannie Mae and Freddie Mac's affordable housing goals proved inefficient and ineffective. Their affordability goals were inadequately responsive to the unique needs of underserved families and communities. They were misaligned with lending in the primary market. And most egregiously, they did not exclude high-cost, predatory loans. As we establish new ways to ensure access and affordability, we must learn from these failed efforts and design policies that are better targeted, more transparent, and focused on providing support that is financially sustainable for families and communities.

We recommend focusing initially on four primary areas of reform:

- A reformed and strengthened FHA.
- A commitment to affordable rental housing.
- Measures to ensure that capital is available to creditworthy borrowers in *all* communities, including rural areas, economically distressed regions, and low-income communities.
- A flexible and transparent funding source to support targeted access and affordability initiatives.

A Reformed and Strengthened FHA

The Administration is committed to ensuring creditworthy first-time homebuyers and families with modest incomes can access a mortgage. The Administration will make sure that creditworthy borrowers that have incomes up to the median level for their area have access to these mortgages, but we will do so in a way that does not allow FHA to expand during normal economic times to a share of the market that is unhealthy or unsustainable.

To make sure that FHA is financially strong enough to provide this key support, and that those taking out FHA-insured single-family loans are taking on sustainable mortgages, the Administration will explore ways to further reduce the risk exposure of FHA. While FHA has already changed its policy to require that borrowers with lower FICO scores put down larger down payments, FHA will consider other options, such as lowering the maximum loan-to-value ratio for qualifying mortgages more broadly. In considering how to apply such options, FHA will continue to balance the need to manage prudently the risk to FHA and the borrower with its efforts to ensure access to affordable loans for lower- and middle-income Americans.

We will work with Congress to give FHA more flexibility to respond to stress in the housing market and manage its risk more effectively. This will mean giving FHA flexibility to adjust fees and programmatic parameters more nimbly than it can today. FHA should also have the technology and talent needed to run what should be a world-class financial institution.

A Renewed Commitment to Affordable Rental Housing

As we move forward to address the challenges of affordability and access, we must address how those issues impact renters. Today, renters often face significant affordability challenges. Half of all renters spend more than a third of their income on housing, and a quarter spend more than half. And for low-income renters, adequate and affordable homes are increasingly scarce. For every 100 extremely low-income American families, for example, only 32 adequate rental homes are affordable.

Promoting a housing finance market that provides liquidity and capital to support affordable rental options can alleviate the high rental burdens that many low-income households face. It can also expand rental options for low-income households in urban, suburban, and rural communities of opportunity, with good jobs for parents and quality schools for children.

Private credit markets have generally underserved multifamily rental properties that offer affordable rents, preferring to invest in high-end developments. By contrast, Fannie Mae and Freddie Mac developed expertise in profitably providing financing to the middle of the rental market, where housing is generally affordable to moderate-income families. As we wind down Fannie Mae and Freddie Mac, it will be critical to find ways to maintain funding to this segment of the market.

The Administration will explore ways to provide greater support for rental housing. One option would be to do so by expanding FHA's capacity to support lending to the multifamily market. Key to this would be utilizing existing multifamily expertise so that FHA and other entities continue the industry's current best practices and retain valuable human capital. We will consider a range of reforms, such as risk-sharing with private lenders, to reduce the risk to FHA and the taxpayer, and the development of programs dedicated to hard-to-reach property segments, including the smaller properties that contain one-third of all rental apartments.

Ensuring that Capital Is Available to Creditworthy Borrowers in All Communities

We will work to ensure that all mortgage market participants are complying with laws that prohibit discrimination in providing capital to borrowers and communities. To support that effort, we will work with Congress to require greater transparency in the mortgage market, requiring securitizers to disclose information on the credit, geographic, and demographic characteristics of the underlying loans they package into securities. This will make it easier to determine whether market participants are complying with their legal obligations, and also make clear to the public what communities these institutions are and are not serving.

We will work with Congress to ensure that *all* communities and families – including those in rural and economically distressed areas, as well as those that are low- and moderate-income – have the access to capital needed for sustainable homeownership and a range of rental options. We will consider measures to make sure that secondary market participants are providing capital to all communities in ways that reflect activity in primary markets, consistent with their obligations of safety and soundness.

Dedicated Funds for Targeted Homeownership and Rental Affordability

Although FHA and other federal affordable housing policies do a great deal to provide access and affordability, we recognize that a more balanced system will require additional resources to address clear gaps. The Administration will thus advocate for a dedicated, budget-neutral financing mechanism to support homeownership and rental housing objectives that current policies cannot adequately address. This funding stream would support the development and preservation of more affordable rental housing for the lowest-income families to address serious supply shortages, similar to the Housing Trust Fund that the President has proposed to be capitalized. It would support down-payment assistance and counseling to help qualified low- and moderate-income homebuyers, in a form that does not expose them or financial institutions to excessive risk or cost. We would scale up support for proven nonprofit partnerships for affordable housing production and preservation that can attract much larger amounts of private capital. And funding would help to overcome market failures that make it hard to develop a secondary market for targeted affordable housing mortgages, such as that for small rental properties.

These components target specific needs in flexible ways that can engage a range of partners and respond to local priorities and opportunities. We will work with Congress to ensure that funding will be budget neutral, transparent, and targeted to clearly defined objectives and programs.

A Responsible Path forward for Reform

The reform measures outlined in this report will help reshape the housing finance market by putting private capital back at the center of a healthier system, reducing taxpayer risk, and increasing protections for consumers and investors. However, given the still-fragile state of the housing market, implementing these reforms fully will take time. The Administration will proceed deliberately so that the mortgage-finance chain and the broader capital markets are not disrupted during this transition.

The Importance of a Responsible Transition

Proceeding with a prudent transition plan and providing the necessary financial support to Fannie Mae and Freddie Mac during that period is essential to protecting the health of the economic recovery and is in the best interests of taxpayers.

A careful transition path offers the best prospects for maximizing recovery on the investments we have made in these institutions and minimizing future losses. Prematurely constraining Fannie Mae and Freddie Mac's ability to guarantee loans or precipitously winding them down could limit the availability of mortgage credit, shock the housing market, and expose taxpayers to additional losses on the loans Fannie Mae and Freddie Mac already guarantee.

The losses that the federal government has covered at Fannie Mae and Freddie Mac under HERA authority are virtually all attributable to bad loans that those firms took on during the height of the housing bubble. Over the last two years, Fannie Mae and Freddie Mac have implemented stricter underwriting standards and increased their pricing. As a result, the new loans being guaranteed by Fannie Mae and Freddie Mac today are of much higher quality than in the past and are unlikely to pose a significant risk of loss to taxpayers.

As Fannie Mae and Freddie Mac are wound down, we must design a transition that allows for continued support of the housing market, so that Americans continue to have the ability to take out a mortgage to buy a home or refinance their existing mortgage. We will continue to work with FHFA to ensure that talent is retained so that mortgage credit continues to flow and risk is contained during the transition, and that the wind down is as successful as possible and supports taxpayers' interests.

The government is committed to ensuring that Fannie Mae and Freddie Mac have sufficient capital to perform under any guarantees issued now or in the future and the ability to meet any of their debt obligations. The Administration will not pursue policies or reforms in a way that would impair the ability of Fannie Mae and Freddie Mac to honor their obligations.

A Path Forward

Determining the appropriate path for how to responsibly wind down Fannie Mae and Freddie Mac and reduce the size of FHA will be challenging and will require great care. As members of the Federal Housing Finance Oversight Board ("FHFOB"), the Advisory Board to FHFA, the Secretaries of Treasury and HUD will make recommendations on the appropriate mix of incentives and deadlines for FHFA to pursue to wind down these institutions at a pace that recognizes the fragile state of the housing market.

We support the creation of a joint FHFA and FHA working group to consider changes to pricing and other standards. We recommend that FHFA and FHA seek comment from the public on the most appropriate pace of the transition and issue a timeline for tightening standards and raising pricing. This working group should provide regular updates to the FHFOB and FSOC, as reforms are implemented. Throughout the transition, FHFA and FHA should continue to seek comment and revise timelines as necessary to account for changing market conditions and accelerate the transition where possible.

As the reforms outlined in the Administration's plan are implemented and new standards at Fannie Mae, Freddie Mac, FHA, and the FHLBs are established, we will ultimately need to complete the transition to a more privatized market. We face a consequential choice about how to structure the government's ultimate role within that market. This report outlines three proposals for Congress and the Administration to consider together. Each of these proposals has unique advantages and disadvantages that deserve thorough evaluation through a robust public dialogue.

Options for the Long-Term Structure of Housing Finance

There has been robust discussion about the long-term future of the American mortgage market and a wide range of options proposed for its reform that differ both in the structure and scale of the government's future role.

As part of this discussion, we considered the range of ways other countries support housing finance. Though there are lessons to be drawn from the diversity of systems, they are complex. In most countries lacking a widely available guarantee or other means of direct government support, mortgages are financed through the banking system, which often enjoys indirect government backing. Some countries utilize their regulatory framework, or establish firm underwriting standards, to promote liquid mortgage markets. And some countries, particularly in Europe, use so-called covered bonds to channel credit to housing.

Like the U.S., several countries have government-supported entities that guarantee or hold mortgages, though in none are they as large as they have historically been in the United States. The U.S. is also the only high-income country in which securitization plays a major role in housing finance. In countries where securitization is present, it generally plays a smaller role and takes different forms than those we are familiar with in this country. The U.S. system, however, is one of the only countries in the world where the majority of mortgages are prepayable, 30-year fixed-rate mortgages.

Although international comparisons offer useful lessons and new ideas, we believe that Americans' housing needs can best be met by a system that takes four key factors into consideration:

Access to Mortgage Credit. Government support for housing finance can expand access to mortgage credit for creditworthy American families. By attracting additional capital into the housing finance system, it can lower the cost of mortgages and increase the availability of certain kinds of mortgage products, such as the 30-year, fixed-rate mortgage. The government can also help standardize the national mortgage market by setting specific criteria for the types of mortgages that it will support. Government support can also increase access to secondary markets for smaller lenders and community banks, promoting a more competitive market and minimizing consolidation.

Incentive for Investment in Housing. Government support makes investment in housing more attractive. While this can broaden access and lower costs for borrowers and communities, it can also draw investment away from other areas that may lead to greater long-term growth or job creation and it can inflate the value of housing assets, possibly leading to larger boom and bust cycles. Without government support, however, some of the capital invested in the housing market today may simply move to investments outside the United States that offer better risk-weighted returns. Other government policies, such as tax incentives like the mortgage interest deduction and other tax credits can also encourage investment towards housing over other sectors in the economy.

Taxpayer Protection. Any time the government stands behind a loan, even indirectly, it takes on some degree of risk. While the government can charge market participants an insurance premium for accepting that risk, pricing risk properly can be difficult. If the government does not charge a fair price, it may encourage excessive risk-taking and increase the likelihood that the taxpayer will be forced to bear the cost of the government's losses. Political pressure to lower the price of government support increases the odds that the government will misprice risk and put taxpayers at risk. Requiring private capital to come ahead of government guarantees or providing a way to ensure taxpayer losses are repaid through future assessments, such as higher fees, may mitigate these risks.

Financial and Economic Stability. Government support can help promote financial stability by ensuring the flow of credit through periods of economic stress. However, if not properly structured, it can also encourage the private market to take on excessive risk and potentially destabilize the system.

While the options that have been proposed vary widely, each can be viewed as posing trade-offs between the four factors mentioned above.

Some advocates and experts have proposed approaches to our housing finance system that starkly illustrate this trade-off: one advocates a near complete privatization of the mortgage market, while others advocate for its near complete nationalization. Under the former, the government would restrict support for the mortgage market to narrowly targeted subsidies for lower-income Americans. Under the latter, the government would provide an explicit guarantee and directly bear most of the credit risk for almost the entire mortgage market.

While each of these approaches has positive attributes, the Administration does not believe that either represents a viable long-term strategy for the nation's housing market. Complete privatization would limit access to, and increase the cost of, mortgages for most Americans too dramatically and leave the government with very little it can do to ensure liquidity during a crisis. Near-complete nationalization runs too high a risk of crowding out private capital, distorting investment decisions, and putting too much taxpayer money at risk.

The Administration believes that the right course falls between these two extremes, with the government's role in the future mortgage market striking a balance between the factors outlined above: creditworthy Americans should have broad access to credit, but not at a cost of excessive taxpayer risk, distorted markets, or financial instability.

With that in mind, we should consider three possible courses for long-term reform.

Option 1: Privatized system of housing finance with the government insurance role limited to FHA, USDA and Department of Veterans' Affairs' assistance for narrowly targeted groups of borrowers

This option would dramatically reduce the government's role in insuring or guaranteeing mortgages, limiting it to FHA and other programs targeted to creditworthy lower- and moderate-income borrowers. While the government would continue to provide access for this targeted segment of borrowers, it would leave the vast majority of the mortgage market to the private sector.

The strength of this option is that it would minimize distortions in capital allocation across sectors, reduce moral hazard in mortgage lending and drastically reduce direct taxpayer exposure to private lenders' losses. With less incentive to invest in housing, more capital will flow into other areas of the economy, potentially leading to more long-run economic growth and reducing the inflationary pressure on housing assets. Risk throughout the system may also be reduced, as private actors will not be as inclined to take on excessive risk without the assurance of a government guarantee behind them. And finally, direct taxpayer risk exposure to private losses in the mortgage market would be limited to the loans guaranteed by FHA and other narrowly-targeted government loan programs: no longer would taxpayers be at direct risk for guarantees covering most of the nation's mortgages.

Though these are indeed significant benefits, this option has particularly acute costs in its potential impact on access to credit for many Americans. While FHA would continue to provide access to mortgage credit for low- and moderate-income Americans, the cost of mortgage credit for those who do not qualify for an FHA-insured loan – the majority of borrowers – would likely increase. While mortgage rates are likely to rise somewhat under any responsible reform proposal, including the three outlined here, the effect could be larger under this option. In particular, it may be more difficult for many

Americans to afford the traditional pre-payable, 30-year fixed-rate mortgage. Additionally, smaller lenders and community banks could have a difficult time competing for business outside of the FHA segment of the market, which may in turn impact access to lending in the communities they have traditionally served more effectively than larger institutions.

Another concern with this option is the ability of the government to effectively step in to ensure access to capital during a crisis. Congress, FHA, the Federal Reserve, and other regulators would be able to play the countercyclical role that they have played in the recent downturn, but it is unlikely that they could play a still more robust role as might be needed in the absence of broader government support in the market. And absent sufficient government support to mitigate a credit crisis, there would be greater risk of a more severe downturn, and thus the risk of greater cost to the taxpayer. A related risk would exist if investors believe that the government would inevitably step in to save whatever private financial institutions or banks have become necessary to maintain the flow of mortgage credit. If so, this option will potentially fail to eliminate the risk of moral hazard.

Option 2: Privatized system of housing finance with assistance from FHA, USDA and Department of Veterans' Affairs for narrowly targeted groups of borrowers and a guarantee mechanism to scale up during times of crisis

As in the option above, FHA and other narrowly targeted programs would provide access to mortgage credit for low- and moderate-income borrowers, but the government's overall role in the housing finance system would be dramatically reduced. In this option, however, the government would also develop a backstop mechanism to ensure access to credit during a housing crisis.

This backstop would maintain a minimal presence in the market during normal times, but would be ready to scale up to a larger share of the market as private capital withdraws in times of financial stress. One approach would be to price the guarantee fee at a sufficiently high level that it would only be competitive in the absence of private capital. It would thus only expand when needed, and that need would be dictated by the market. An alternative approach would restrict the amount of public insurance sold to the private market in normal times, but allow the amount of insurance offered to ramp up to stabilize the market in times of stress.

The strength of this proposal is that it would be designed to address one of the primary concerns associated with the prior model – the inability of the government to soften a contraction of credit during a crisis – without necessarily taking on all the costs associated with a broad government guarantee during normal times. During normal times it would avoid the distortions in the housing market associated with a broad-based guarantee and thus reduce both moral hazard and taxpayer risk. Again, private capital would be more likely to flow to the most productive assets in the economy, private actors would be on the hook for their own risky decisions and the government would not be putting taxpayers at direct risk in backing the nation's mortgage market.

In addition to these benefits, the government would be in a better position than under Option One to manage another downturn in the housing market. As private capital pulls back, the government could better step in to ensure the availability of credit and thus help to stabilize a declining market. Though this would likely be more effective than relying only on Congress, FHA, and the Federal Reserve, there remains a significant operational challenge in designing and managing an organization that can remain small during normal economic times, yet has the capacity to take on much more business quickly during these times of need.

There are other costs to this model as well. Aside from the uncertainty around how well it would be able to scale up in times of crisis, there is the same concern with the access issues that we face with the prior option. Access to credit, particularly the pre-payable, 30-year fixed-rate mortgage, would likely be more expensive under this option than under the following one.

Option 3: Privatized system of housing finance with FHA, USDA and Department of Veterans' Affairs assistance for low- and moderate-income borrowers and catastrophic reinsurance behind significant private capital

Under this option, as in the previous options, the mortgage market outside of the FHA and other federal agency guarantee programs would be driven by private investment decisions with private capital taking the primary credit risk. However, to increase the liquidity in the mortgage market and access to mortgages for creditworthy Americans – as well as to ensure the government's ability to respond to future crises – the government would offer reinsurance for the securities of a targeted range of mortgages.

In one approach to such a system, a group of private mortgage guarantor companies that meet stringent capital and oversight requirements would provide guarantees for securities backed by mortgages that meet strict underwriting standards. A government reinsurer would then provide reinsurance to the holders of these securities, which would be paid out only if shareholders of the private mortgage guarantors have been entirely wiped out. The government reinsurer would charge a premium for this reinsurance, which would be used to cover future claims and recoup losses to protect taxpayers.

The strength of this option is that it likely provides the lowest-cost access to mortgage credit of the three options. While mortgage rates would be increased by the cost of the premium and the first-loss position of private capital, this reinsurance will likely attract a larger pool of investors to the mortgage market, increasing liquidity. This, in turn, could help to lower the prices and pricing volatility of mortgages and increase the availability of the pre-payable, 30-year fixed-rate mortgage. It will also provide a more competitive playing field for smaller lenders and community banks, which, in turn, could improve access in communities where those institutions have a good record of service. And finally, the government reinsurer's broad presence in the market could put it in a position to scale up to provide credit during a time of stress in the market more effectively.

However, this option, too, comes with costs. The increased flow of capital into the mortgage market could draw capital away from potentially more productive sectors of the economy and could artificially inflate the value of housing assets. And while the capital requirements, oversight of the private mortgage guarantors, and premiums collected to cover future losses will together help to reduce the risk to the taxpayer, the reinsurance of private-lending activity, by its nature, exposes the government to risk and moral hazard. If the oversight of the private mortgage guarantors is inadequate or the pricing of the reinsurance too low or recoupment of costs too politically difficult, then private actors in the market may take on excessive risk and the taxpayer could again bear the cost.

THE CHOICE AHEAD

In choosing among these options, care must be given to designing a system that maximizes the benefits we are seeking from government involvement in the mortgage market, while minimizing the costs. We must also consider how to utilize the existing systems and assets in our housing finance system, including those at Fannie Mae and Freddie Mac, as best as possible for the benefit of the taxpayer and the American people. But design choices alone will not tell us what the best path is for the future of our mortgage system, for we are faced with difficult trade-offs. We must decide what we take to be the right balance between providing broad access to mortgages for American families, managing the risk to taxpayers, and maintaining a stable and healthy mortgage market. As we see above, these priorities are not always well aligned, so we will have to make difficult decisions as we choose the path for long-term reform.

There will of course be significant debate about how to strike this difficult balance. But we must be careful not to let that debate keep us from the immediate task at hand: we need to scale back the role of government in the mortgage market, and promote the return of private capital to a healthier, more robust mortgage market.

We will continue to seek input and consult with a wide variety of constituents, market participants, academic experts, and consumer and community organizations on our plan for reform. Given the importance of the long-term stability of the housing market and the critical role the government continues to play in the current financial circumstances, this approach to housing finance reform, built upon significant input from various stakeholders, should form the basis for a strong bi-partisan solution that results in a stronger housing finance market for all Americans.

The housing finance system *must* be reformed. It is the vital link to sustainable homeownership and rental options for millions of Americans, and it is central to our nation's economy. We allowed its flaws to go unchecked for too long, contributing to a financial collapse that has strained families, decimated communities, and pushed the economy into the worst recession since the Great Depression. The Obama Administration here provides a path of reform, which will lead to a future system with more private capital, better-aligned incentives, more oversight, and less risk to the taxpayer – in short, to a healthier, more stable system of housing finance.

Housing Finance Reform in America
Editors: B. W. Virtanen, E. A. Laine ISBN: 978-1-61324-350-3

Chapter 2

FANNIE MAE'S AND FREDDIE MAC'S FINANCIAL PROBLEMS*

N. Eric Weiss

SUMMARY

The conservatorship of Fannie Mae and Freddie Mac raises questions about the impact of these government-sponsored enterprises (GSEs) on the housing and finance markets and their ability to return to financial viability. To date, the federal government has purchased more than $148 billion in stock in the two companies, with pending requests from Fannie Mae to purchase an additional $2.5 billion and from Freddie Mac for $100 million. Once these transactions are completed, the Treasury will hold $152.8 billion in senior preferred stock. Both companies are required under terms of the federal support to pay the government dividends of more than $15 billion annually (10% of the support). Housing, mortgage, and even general financial markets remain in an unprecedented situation.

Estimates of the total cost to the federal government use different baselines and vary widely. The Federal Housing Finance Agency (FHFA) estimates that Treasury is likely to purchase $221 billion–$363 billion of senior preferred stock by the end of 2013. The Congressional Budget Office estimates the budget cost for 2011-2020 to be $53 billion. Standard & Poor's has estimated the cost at $280 billion plus $405 billion to create a replacement system.

---

* This is an edited, reformatted and augmented version of a Congressional Research Services publication, dated December 20, 2010.

Once Treasury's support for Fannie Mae and Freddie Mac ends, sometime after 2012, they will be challenged to pay the 10% annual cash dividend contained in their contracts. The enterprises could instead pay a 12% annual senior preferred stock dividend indefinitely.

FHFA placed Fannie Mae and Freddie Mac into conservatorship after turmoil in the housing, mortgage, and financial markets raised doubts about the future of these enterprises, which are chartered by Congress as GSEs and whose debts are widely believed to be implicitly guaranteed by the federal government. The FHFA replaced the Office of Federal Housing Enterprise Oversight (OFHEO) as the GSEs' safety and soundness regulator. OFHEO repeatedly assured investors that Fannie and Freddie had adequate capital, but as highly leveraged financial intermediaries, Fannie Mae and Freddie Mac had limited capital to cushion themselves against losses.

The Treasury agreed to buy mortgage-backed securities (MBSs) from the GSEs and to raise funds for them. Initially, each GSE gave Treasury $1 billion in senior preferred stock and warrants to acquire, at nominal cost, 80% of each GSE. When Treasury responds to the GSEs' request for additional funds for the third quarter of 2010, it will hold nearly $153 billion of preferred stock in the two GSEs. Treasury has agreed to invest whatever is required to maintain GSE solvency through calendar year 2012. Now the formerly implicit guarantee is nearly explicit.

In addition to Treasury's purchases of senior preferred stock, the Federal Reserve (Fed) has purchased GSE bonds and MBSs. According to a November 9, 2010, FHFA report, together the Fed and Treasury have purchased $1,356.7 billion in MBSs; these purchase programs terminated at the end of the first quarter of 2010.

INTRODUCTION

This report presents, in analytical question and answer form, the issues surrounding the financial conditions of Fannie Mae and Freddie Mac, which are stockholder-owned government-sponsored enterprises (GSEs). Their federal charters give the GSEs special public policy goals to provide liquidity in the mortgage market and to provide access to homeownership for underserved groups and locations. In return, their charters give the GSEs a special relationship with the government.

On September 7, 2008, the federal government took control of the GSEs from their stockholders and management in a process known as conservatorship. The goal of conservatorship is to restore the GSEs' financial strength and to return control to their stockholders and management. Conservatorship is discussed in more detail later in this report.

A glossary of terms is included at the end of this report.

FANNIE MAE'S AND FREDDIE MAC'S CURRENT STATUS

What Is the Current Financial Condition of Fannie Mae and Freddie Mac?

In the first three quarters of 2010, Fannie Mae and Freddie Mac reported the continuation of losses that had started in the third quarter of 2007, interrupted only by Freddie Mac's profit in the second quarter of 2009. Neither GSE has had a profitable year since 2006. These losses are notable because previously the GSEs had been consistently profitable. Fannie Mae had not reported a full-year loss since 1985, and Freddie Mac had never reported a full-year loss since it became stockholder owned.[1]

Table 1 summarizes the losses and profits of Fannie Mae and Freddie Mac since 2006. They started 2006 earning quarterly profits, but lost money in the third quarter (July, August, and September). They were profitable for the entire year of 2006 and the first two quarters of 2007. For the entire year of 2007, the two GSEs reported combined losses of slightly less than $5.2 billion. For the entire year of 2008, the two GSEs reported combined losses of slightly less than $109 billion. For the entire year of 2009, Fannie Mae reported losses of $72 billion and Freddie Mac reported losses of $21.6 billion. Both GSEs reported losses in the first three quarters of 2010.

Two major sources of losses for mortgage lenders, including the GSEs, have been loans to borrowers with less than prime credit (subprime) and certain types of mortgages to borrowers with credit between prime and subprime (Alt-A). Fannie Mae held $24.6 billion in private-label mortgage-backed securities (MBSs) backed by subprime mortgages; it held $27.9 billion in private-label MBSs backed by Alt-A mortgages.[2] Freddie Mac held $74.9 billion in private-label MBSs backed by subprime mortgages and $25.1 billion in private-label MBSs backed by Alt-A mortgages.[3] The GSEs have, in addition, increased loan loss reserves in anticipation of continuing losses. If losses on foreclosed mortgages are less than predicted, the reserves could be reduced, which would improve the GSEs' financial condition.

To make certain that the GSEs have adequate funds to cover potential losses, the Federal Housing Finance Agency (FHFA), like all financial safety and soundness regulators, imposes capital requirements. At the end of 2007, the two GSEs had a $24.8 billion surplus more than the regulatory capital requirement of $58.4 billion; they had a surplus of $50.8 billion more than the risk-based capital requirement of $38.8 billion.[4] At the end of 2008, Fannie Mae had a minimum capital requirement deficit of $42.1 billion and Freddie Mac had minimum capital requirement deficit of $41.4 billion.[5] FHFA has said that it will not calculate risk based capital requirements while the GSEs are in conservatorship.

Table 1. GSE Profitability Since 2006 ($ in millions).

Quarter	Fannie Mae	Freddie Mac
1st Quarter 2006	$2,026	$1,942
2nd Quarter 2006	2,058	1,336
3rd Quarter 2006	–629	–550
4th Quarter 2006	604	401
Full Year 2006	4,059	2,327
1st Quarter 2007	961	–133
2nd Quarter 2007	1,947	729
3rd Quarter 2007	–1,399	–1,238
4th Quarter 2007	–3,559	–2,452
Full Year 2007	–2,050	–3,094
1st Quarter 2008	–2,186	–151
2nd Quarter 2008	–2,300	–821
3rd Quarter 2008	–28,994	–25,295
4th Quarter 2008	–25,227	–23,852
Full Year 2008	–58,707	–50,119
1st Quarter 2009	–23,168	–9,975
2nd Quarter 2009	–14,754	302
3rd Quarter 2009	–18,872	–5,408
4th Quarter 2009	–15,175	–6,472
Full Year 2009	–71,969	–21,553
1st Quarter 2010	–11,530	–6,688
2nd Quarter 2010	-1,218	-4,713
3rd Quarter 2010	-1,339	-2,511

Source: Fannie Mae (httpi/www.fanniemae.com/ir/) and Freddie Mac (httpi/www.freddiemac.com/investors

Note: Freddie Mac's 2009 annual report revised previously released 2009 quarterly net income. This table reflects the revisions. Amounts shown are "net loss attributable to Fannie Mae," and "net loss attributable to Freddie Mac," which exclude dividends paid to Treasury on the senior preferred stock. All other dividends have been suspended.

To meet their capital requirements, the GSEs could either reduce their needed capital by selling some mortgages and MBSs from their portfolios, or raise new capital from investors. They have been unable or unwilling to take either of these alternatives. Instead, they have sold additional preferred stock to the Treasury.

Since the third quarter of 2008, FHFA, as conservator of the GSEs, has asked Treasury for a total of $87.6 billion to increase Fannie Mae's assets to offset its liabilities and a total of $63.2 billion for Freddie Mac. The third quarter 2010 requests for $2.5 billion and $100 million, respectively, are pending. Technically, Treasury support for the GSEs comes through purchases of GSE senior preferred stock. **Table 2** reports the amounts, including the $1 billion of senior preferred stock that each GSE gave Treasury when they were taken into conservatorship. This stock is senior to (has priority over) all other common and preferred stock; it is the only stock currently receiving dividends.

Table 2. Treasury Holdings of GSE Senior Preferred Stock ($ in millions).

	Fannie Mae	Freddie Mac
Initial Agreement (No explicit cost)	$1,000	$1,000
3rd Quarter 2008	0	13,800
4th Quarter 2008	15,200	30,800
Year 2008	16,200	45,600
1st Quarter 2009	19,000	6,100
2nd Quarter 2009	10,700	0
3rd Quarter 2009	15,000	0
4th Quarter 2009	15,300	0
Year 2009	60,000	6,100
1st Quarter 2010	8,400	10,600
2nd Quarter 2010	1,500	1,800
3rd Quarter 2010	2,500	100
Total Holdings	$88,600	$64,200

Source: Fannie Mae (httpi/www.fanniemae.com/ir/) and Freddie Mac (httpi/www.freddiemac.com/investors

Note: Each "total holdings" includes $1 billion in senior preferred stock that the GSEs gave Treasury at the time of their conservatorship agreements.

In addition to Treasury's purchases of senior preferred stock, the Federal Reserve (Fed) has purchased GSE bonds and MBSs. According to a November 9, 2010, FHFA report, together the Fed and Treasury have purchased $1,356.7 billion in MBSs.[6]

Can the GSEs Continue to Pay Dividends to Treasury?

Under terms of the support contracts that the GSEs individually signed with Treasury, each is required to pay annually either 10% cash dividends or 12% stock dividends on the senior preferred stock issued to Treasury. As of the end of the third quarter of 2010, this requires Fannie Mae to pay annually either $8.9 billion in cash or $10.6 billion in stock and Freddie Mac to pay either $6.4 billion in cash or $7.7 billion in stock. Fannie Mae has never earned enough in any single year to make its dividend payments in cash; Freddie Mac earned enough only once—in 2002.[7] Consequently, once the GSEs no longer are receiving financial support from Treasury, the GSEs would have to be more profitable than they ever have been for them to make more than one year of cash dividend payments. This is made less likely by provisions in the contracts requiring the GSEs to reduce the size of their mortgage portfolios, which in recent years the GSEs increased to increase their profits.

Without Treasury's support, a GSE lacking the funds to pay the cash dividend could pay the 12% dividend in additional senior preferred stock. It appears that this could continue indefinitely unless Congress were to pass legislation modifying the GSE's charter, Treasury were to take control of the GSE by exercising its warrants to purchase 79.9% of the GSE's common stock, or FHFA as conservator were to act.

Why Did Fannie Mae Attempt to Sell Low-Income Housing Tax Credits?

Fannie Mae's quarterly report for the third quarter of 2009 reported that the company was seeking the government's permission to sell approximately $2.6 billion in Low-Income Housing Tax Credits (LIHTC). The credits had little or no value to Fannie Mae because the GSE is not likely to incur any tax liabilities in the foreseeable future. FHFA approved the sale as "conserve Enterprise assets and with the Enterprise's multifamily housing mission."[8]

Under its senior preferred stock agreement, Fannie Mae was required to obtain Treasury's approval to dispose of these assets. Treasury denied the request as being too costly for taxpayers: Fannie Mae is very unlikely to earn enough income to pay taxes, making the tax credits useless to Fannie Mae and costless to Treasury.[9] Any company purchasing the credits would do so to reduce its taxes reducing Treasury's tax revenues.

Freddie Mac has stated that in light of the Treasury decision about Fannie Mae, it will not request permission to sell its LIHTC.

What Is Happening to Fannie Mae's and Freddie Mac's Affordable Housing Initiatives?

FHFA announced new goals and revised procedures for scoring Fannie Mae's and Freddie Mac's success in reaching the housing goals.[10] In particular, Home Ownership Equity Protection Act (HOEPA) mortgages, second mortgages, mortgages with original balances above the conforming loan limit, mortgages with interest rates 300 basis points (3%) or more above the applicable average prime offer rates as reported in the Home Mortgage Disclosure Act (HMDA) data, and mortgages with missing information necessary to determine compliance with the goals would be excluded.[11] Fannie Mae and Freddie Mac can also meet their housing goals by purchasing mortgages such that their goal and subgoal percentages equal or exceed the market percentage. **Table 3** summarizes the 2010 and 2011 housing goals and subgoals.

FHFA reduced the 2010 multifamily goals. For 2009, FHFA reduced the GSEs' low-income, underserved areas, and special affordable single-family housing goals to the 2008 targets.[12]

Fannie Mae reported that it exceeded the underserved areas goal, but did not reach the two others in 2008. Freddie Mac reported that it did not reach any of the three goals in 2008. Neither Fannie Mae nor Freddie Mac reported reaching the home purchase subgoals in 2008.

In contrast to its action with the GSEs' 2009 single family goals, FHFA increased the special affordable multifamily goal for 2009 compared with the 2008 levels, which both GSEs exceeded. **Table 4** summarizes the 2009 housing goals.

Table 3. GSE 2010-2011 Housing Goals and Subgoals.

Category	Goal/Subgoal	2010-2011 Goal
Low-Income Families Housing Goal	Goal	27% purchase money
Very Low-Income Families Housing Goal	Goal	8% purchase money
Low-Income Areas Housing Goal	Goal	13% purchase money
Refinancing Housing Goal	Goal	21% refinance
Multifamily Low-Income Housing Goal	Fannie Mae Freddie Mac	177,750 dwelling units 161,250 dwelling units
Multifamily Very Low-Income Housing Subgoal	Fannie Mae	42,750 dwelling units
	Freddie Mac	21,000 dwelling units

Source: U.S. Federal Housing Finance Agency, "2010–2011 Enterprise Housing Goals; Enterprise Book-entry Procedures," 75 *Federal Register* 55892-55939, September 14, 2010.

Notes: Alternatively, Fannie Mae and Freddie Mac can meet their housing goals by purchasing mortgages such that their goal/subgoals percentages equal or exceed the market percentage.

Table 4. GSE 2009 Housing Goals.

Category	Goal/Subgoal	Goal/Subgoal 2008	Fannie Mae Performance 2008	Freddie Mac Performance 2008	2009 Goal
Low-Mod Income	Goal	56%	53.7%	51.5%	43%
Underserved Areas	Goal	39%	39.4%	37.7%	32%
Special Affordable	Goal	27%	26.4%	23.1%	18%
Low-Mod Income	Home Purchase Subgoal	47%	38.8%	39.3%	40%
Underserved Areas	Home Purchase Subgoal	34%	30.4%	30.3%	30%
Special Affordable	Home Purchase Subgoal	18%	13.6%	15.1%	14%
Special Affordable	Fannie Mae	$5.49 billion	$13.43 billion		$6.56 billion
Multifamily	Freddie Mac	$3.92 billion		$7.68 billion	$4.60 billion

Source: U.S. Federal Housing Finance Agency, "2009 Enterprise Transition Affordable Housing Goals," 74 *Federal Register* 39873-39900, August 10, 2009 and U.S. Federal Housing Finance Agency, "The Housing Goals of Fannie Mae and Freddie Mac in the Context of the Mortgage Market: 1996 – 2009," Mortgage Market Note 10-2, February 1, 2010.

Do Fannie Mae and Freddie Mac Have Any Programs to Help Mortgage Borrowers?

Fannie Mae and Freddie Mac each have two special programs for mortgage borrowers, but only for borrowers whose loans each holds. The Home Affordable Loan Modification program is for borrowers who are delinquent on their mortgages. The Home Affordable Refinance is for borrowers who are current on their mortgages and want to refinance to a lower interest rate. Both programs have certain eligibility and qualification requirements. The programs are being administered by the borrower's current mortgage servicer. Information on these programs is available at http://www.makinghomeaffordable.gov/.

The GSEs' refinance programs differ in terms of interest rates and fees.

Fannie Mae and Freddie Mac have programs to allow a homeowner facing foreclosure to surrender the deed-in-lieu of foreclosure and then to lease the home back. The Fannie Mae lease is for 12 months and can be renewed, whereas the Freddie Mac lease is month-to-month. Both programs charge a market rate for the lease.

Who Manages the GSEs?

Fannie Mae and Freddie Mac have separate management teams headed by a chief executive officer (CEO) and overseen by their conservator and regulator, the Federal Housing Finance Agency. Fannie Mae CEO Daniel H. Mudd and Freddie Mac CEO Richard F. Syron resigned when their companies were placed in conservatorship on September 7, 2008. FHFA appointed Herbert M. Allison, Jr. as Fannie Mae's CEO and David Moffett as Freddie Mac's CEO.

Effective March 13, 2009, Moffett resigned from Freddie Mac to return to the private sector. He has since returned as a consultant. On April 20, 2009, Allison resigned from Fannie Mae to accept the nomination to be Assistant Treasury Secretary for Financial Stability (who oversees Treasury's Troubled Asset Relief Program) and Counselor to the Secretary.

Freddie Mac appointed Charles E. Haldeman, Jr. as CEO to succeed Moffett, and Fannie Mae appointed Michael J. Williams as president and CEO to succeed Allison.

There have been press reports to the effect that many senior executives at the GSEs have found it difficult to manage their companies under conservatorship.[13]

What Is Happening to Executive Compensation?

The Housing and Economic Recovery Act strengthened FHFA's regulation over executive compensation and golden parachutes. The senior preferred stock agreement signed by each GSE with FHFA requires the GSEs to get approval for new compensation agreements with executives.

On December 22, 2009, Fannie Mae and Freddie Mac announced that FHFA had approved 2010 compensation packages for their chief executive officers of $6 million each.[14] This consists of base pay ($900,000 each), deferred pay ($3.1 million), and long-term incentive pay ($2 million). Six other Fannie Mae executives and four other Freddie Mac executives are covered by this system, but will receive lesser amounts. The deferred pay will weight performance and service equally, and it will be paid quarterly in 2011. The long-term incentive pay will vary according to individual and corporate performance; 50% will be paid in 2011 and the remaining 50% will be paid in 2012.

In March 2009, Representative Barney Frank, chairman of the House Financial Services Committee, wrote to FHFA Director James Lockhart asking that retention for bonuses for staff, including executives, at Fannie Mae and Freddie Mac be rescinded; Director Lockhart allowed the bonuses to be paid.[15]

After accounting irregularities were uncovered in 2003 and 2004, OFHEO sued Fannie Mae's and Freddie Mac's previous CEOs (Franklin D. Raines and Leland C. Brendsel, respectively) to recover part of their compensation; in both cases, out of court settlements were reached, which included the payment of fines and donations to charities.

What Risks Do Fannie Mae's and Freddie Mac's Financial Problems Create for Homeowners and Those Planning to Become Homeowners?

Fannie Mae's and Freddie Mac's financial problems create no risks for homeowners who want to stay in their homes and who do not want to refinance. Homeowners continue to pay their existing mortgages.

Treasury's actions of lending money to the GSEs and the Fed's purchases of MBSs from the GSEs should help to stabilize the secondary mortgage market and provide a continuing flow of funds to purchase new homes and to refinance existing mortgages. In 2007, the GSEs financed 91.3% of the conforming mortgage market, and their 2008 market share was 97.8%.[16]

Under conservatorship, the GSEs have become active in loan modifications and refinancing existing mortgages that they own. They have become more cautious about the mortgages that they purchase, with stricter underwriting rules and higher fees. These actions are similar to other lenders' behavior in the current recession and previous economic slowdowns.

The Economic Stimulus Act of 2008 (ESA) raised the loan limit for Federal Housing Administration (FHA) guaranteed loans in most high-cost areas of the nation to the same maximum that the GSEs are permitted to purchase.[17] As a result, FHA-guaranteed loans can, in theory, replace most conventional loans.

What Risks Do Fannie Mae and Freddie Mac Face in Today's Economic Environment?

In any economic environment Fannie Mae and Freddie Mac face a variety of risks that many other companies face. The GSEs purchase home mortgages. They package most mortgages into MBSs, selling some and holding others in their investment portfolios. The GSEs finance their portfolios of long-term (typically 30-year) mortgages with short-term borrowing (typically three months to five years). This increases the GSEs' profits because short-term borrowing is usually less expensive than longer term loans. At the same time, this creates *interest rate risk*, which is the risk that if short-term interest rates increase, profitability can be reduced or can even turn to losses. For example, if interest rates were to increase to 6%, mortgages at 5% would not be profitable.[18] To try to reduce these risks, the GSEs use a variety of financial derivatives.[19]

In a worst case scenario, the interest rate on short-term loans to the GSEs could increase enough to cause substantial losses and investors could stop entering into derivative contracts with the GSEs. This would leave the GSEs, who anticipated being able to roll over their short-term debt, unable to refinance. Treasury's financial promises of a GSE Credit Facility (GSECF) and purchasing MBSs greatly reduce this risk.

The GSEs are subject to *credit risk*. The GSEs guarantee timely payment of principal and interest of the mortgages in their MBSs. As mortgage foreclosure rates have climbed since 2006, and as home prices have fallen, the value of the mortgages and MBSs that the two firms hold in their portfolio has also fallen. Uncertainty about the duration and severity of the housing slump means that markets cannot now gauge the riskiness of the GSEs with much confidence or precision. The Treasury's support has reduced this risk, but it is not clear if stockholders will benefit.

Like all other businesses, the GSEs have *operational risk* due to the failure of internal controls.

FHFA has directed the GSEs to reduce operational risk by improving their information technology, data quality, and internal controls.

As financial corporations, the GSEs are also subject to *model risk*, or the risk that their models (especially credit models) are not accurate. FHFA has directed the GSEs to update their financial models to reflect changing conditions.

What Is the Federal Government's Potential Contribution?

To keep the GSEs solvent from 2010 through 2012, Treasury has agreed to purchase as much senior preferred stock as necessary.[20]

Treasury initially had agreed to purchase a maximum of $100 billion in senior preferred stock from each GSE, and later increased the $100 billion to $200 billion.

After 2012, any unused portions of the $200 billion could be used. Treasury's authority to amend the contracts expired December 31, 2009.[21]

Upon entering conservatorship (September 7, 2008), each GSE issued Treasury $1 billion of senior preferred stock and warrants (options) to purchase common stock. If the warrants are exercised, Treasury would own 79.9% of each company. As part of the contracts, each GSE has agreed to restrictions on paying dividends, issuing new stock, and disposing of assets.

At the same time as it increased its potential GSE support, Treasury increased the maximum retained portfolio that each GSE can hold. The maximum amount for each GSE is $900 billion as of December 31, 2009, and this maximum decreases by 10% annually until it reaches $250 billion. At this rate, it will take more than 12 years to reduce a GSE's portfolio to $250 billion. Previously, the ceiling was the actual size of the portfolio on December 31, 2009. By way of reference, the most current information available (for the end of November 2009) is that Fannie Mae's retained mortgage portfolio was $752 billion and Freddie Mac's retained portfolio was $762 billion.

The December 24, 2009, announcement said that Treasury would terminate its program to purchase MBS of GSEs at the end of the year. Treasury estimated that at year end it would hold approximately $220 billion in MBS.[22] Treasury has said that it expects to profit from the spread between the interest rate that it pays to borrow money through bonds and the mortgage payments on the MBSs. Separately, the New York Federal Reserve has its own program to purchase a maximum of $1.25 trillion of GSE MBSs.[23] The GSEs will guarantee payment of the MBSs.

Treasury created a Government Sponsored Enterprise Credit Facility (GSECF) to provide liquidity to the GSEs, secured by MBSs pledged as collateral.[24] This facility terminated December 31, 2009.

Estimates of the total cost to the federal government use different baselines and vary widely. FHFA has estimated that by the end of 2013, Treasury is likely to purchase $221 billion-$363 billion of senior preferred stock[25] and the Congressional Budget Office has estimated the budget cost for 2011-2020 to be $53 billion.[26] Standard & Poor has estimated that the total cost to resolve the GSEs could be $280 billion and that it would cost another $405 billion to capitalize a new entity or entities to replace Fannie Mae and Freddie Mac.[27]

What Risks Do Fannie Mae and Freddie Mac Create for the U.S. Government?

In the event of receivership, the usual priority of claims on remaining assets is administrative expenses of the receivership, senior and general debt, subordinated debt, and stock.[28] This would seem to place the MBSs with their guarantee at a fairly senior position, followed by GSE bonds, which would be ahead of the government's senior preferred stock, which would be ahead of all other stockholders.

If a GSE were to go into receivership, the value of its MBSs could decline because the value of the guarantee of timely payment of the MBSs would be called into question. If the GSE were unable to perform on the timely payment guarantee, the value of the MBSs would depend on the payment of the underlying mortgages, the rules of receivership, and the government's support for the MBSs.

The eventual value of the bonds would depend on the cause of the receivership and the details of the liquidation process. For example, if mortgage defaults and losses were to increase, the assets available for creditors would decrease.

In the event of receivership, it would appear unlikely that the senior preferred stock would have much value.

What is the Difference Between the Housing and Economic Recovery Act of 2008 and the Federal Housing Finance Regulatory Reform Act of 2008?

The Housing and Economic Recovery Act of 2008 is the title for the entire law, P.L. 110-289. The Federal Housing Finance Regulatory Reform Act of 2008 is the title for Title I-III of P.L. 110- 289.

FUTURE

Could the GSEs Continue as Before?

In principle, Congress might decide that the changes that FHFA is making to each of the GSEs reduce the risk of future financial problems to an acceptable level and that the GSEs could return to stockholder control.[29]

The federal government's financial support extended to the GSEs could make a return to the prior status problematic. The elimination of dividends greatly reduced the value of the GSEs' preferred stock. Because the appeal of preferred stock is centered on the security of the dividend payments, the long-run value of their preferred stock has been reduced. The value of common stock has been reduced because of the termination of their dividends and increased uncertainty over the future long-run viability of the enterprises. Even if the GSEs were to return to stockholder control, it is not clear how much appeal their common and preferred stock would have for investors. If the GSEs were unable to raise capital, they would be unable to continue.

The treatment of bond holders could make lending to the GSEs more attractive. While common and preferred stockholders suffered during conservatorship (but not as much as they would have suffered from dissolution of the GSEs), payments to bond and MBS holders have continued as contracted. The government's actions could convince bondholders that the risk of holding bonds is less than previously thought. This would allow the GSEs to borrow money by selling bonds at rates very close to Treasury rates.

The increasing defaults and loss severity probably has made MBSs appear more risky, but the government's support of the GSEs could have offset this.

Once the current recession is over, the GSEs could be in a very strong position to purchase mortgages and to create MBSs. For stockholders, the economics of the GSEs' mortgage business could be attractive, but the psychology of the decline in stock prices and the dividends on the senior preferred stock could potentially offset this plus.

One open question in the GSEs' return to stockholder ownership is the government's decision on what to do with the warrants for 80% of the GSEs' ownership. The government could auction the warrants off to the highest bidder, or the government could exercise the warrants to obtain control of the GSEs as each one's majority stockholder.

What Are Some of Congress's Options for Restructuring the GSEs?

Going forward, Congress has many options for reorganizing Fannie Mae and Freddie Mac, including (but not limited to) the following:

- Congress could make Fannie Mae and Freddie Mac part of the government. Both GSEs were originally government corporations, and this would be a return to that environment.
- Fannie Mae and Freddie Mac could become Federal Home Loan Banks. The 12 regional banks are a collective GSE that is owned by their member institutions, and their stock is not publicly traded. Fannie Mae's and Freddie Mac's stock could become an asset of the Federal Home Loan Bank System or of the individual banks.
- Fannie Mae and Freddie Mac could be split up into a large number of GSEs. Instead of two GSEs that are "too big to fail," there would be 10 or some other number of smaller GSEs that would arguably each be small enough to fail. The GSEs could be split in such a way that they would not be clones of each other and one or two could fail without the others going under. Congress might wish to explicitly

state what the risks to stockholders, bondholders, and business partners would be. The competition could mean more benefits from GSE status go to home buyers instead of the GSEs.

- Fannie Mae and Freddie Mac (and possibly additional new GSEs) could be converted into "utilities." These corporations would not necessarily be GSEs. Each could issue MBSs possibly guaranteed by the federal government, which would charge a fee for the guarantee. There are a number of options for how the fees could be set. The government could establish a standard fee, or it could auction off the right to issue a specific amount of MBSs. They could sell these MBSs or possibly retain them.
- The government could sell additional new GSE charters to the highest bidders.
- As Treasury Secretary, Henry M. Paulson, Jr., proposed using bonds backed not only by the issuing corporation's legal obligation of repayment, but also by the pledge of specific collateral as a way to allow banks to supplement, or even replace, the GSEs' role in mortgage markets.[30]

What Has Conservatorship Done to Stockholders and Other Stakeholders?

The powers of common stockholders, who formerly elected the boards of directors and approved certain enterprise actions, are suspended. FHFA as the conservator has assumed all of their authority. Previously, the common stockholders owned 100% of the GSEs. As a result of the warrants issued to the Treasury, they could own only 20% of the enterprises. In the long run, 20% of a healthy enterprise could be worth more than 100% of GSEs whose liabilities exceed their assets. In the short run, the price of the GSEs' common stock has declined, but if the GSEs recover, stockholders would arguably be better off compared to their situation at the time that conservatorship was undertaken.

To the extent that current and former employees have invested in common stock, in the short run they have seen a decline in the value of their financial assets; the long-run outcome is not clear. Both GSEs had employee stock and option plans. The GSEs' agreements with Treasury prohibit issuing new stock. Consequently those programs cannot continue until the GSEs emerge from conservatorship.

GSE employees, except for the CEO of each enterprise, are being urged by FHFA to continue working as before. The CEOs have been replaced, but they agreed to assist in the transition. Employees may decide to look for other employment, but they generally have the option to stay.

While the conservator is authorized by federal law to cancel certain contracts, FHFA has said that current contracts continue in force.

Treasury has purchased special senior preferred stock from Fannie Mae and Freddie Mac to maintain assets greater than liabilities. This senior preferred stock pays annual dividends of 10%, which would increase to 12% annually if a GSE fails to pay the dividend; these are the only dividends that the GSEs are allowed to pay. To date, the GSEs have increased the amount of preferred stock sold to Treasury to pay the dividends.

How Can Fannie Mae and Freddie Mac Leave Conservatorship?

There are two ways that Fannie Mae and Freddie Mac could exit their conservatorships. If they become financially viable, they could return to stockholder control. If they are unable to become financially viable, they could enter receivership. There is no legal reason that one GSE could not go into receivership and the other GSE return to stockholder control, although this might present some policy questions about the desirability of having a monopoly GSE.

There are several obstacles to a return to financial viability. In conservatorship, the GSEs are balancing their goals of support for home mortgage markets and their goal of profitability. Many times these goals conflict. The concern of the federal government and FHFA for mortgage market stability and liquidity may take precedence over the return to profitability.[31]

The 10% cash or 12% senior preferred stock dividends owed to the federal government could be burdensome. The annual cash dividends of this stock equal or exceed the profits that the GSEs have earned in most years since 1998. This suggests that it could be difficult if not impossible for the GSEs to pay the required dividends without Treasury's continued financial support.

CONTEXT

What Is Conservatorship?

Conservatorship of Fannie Mae and Freddie Mac involves FHFA taking control of the GSEs. As conservator, the powers of the board of directors, officers, and shareholders are transferred to FHFA. A conservator can also cancel certain contracts. This is authorized by the Housing and Economic Recovery Act of 2008 (HERA).[32] The goal of conservatorship is to preserve the GSE's assets and to return it to sound financial condition that would allow the conservatorship to be ended.

FHFA replaced the existing CEOs of Fannie Mae and Freddie Mac.

Why Did the FHFA Place Fannie Mae and Freddie Mac Under Conservatorship?

As regulator of Fannie Mae and Freddie Mac, FHFA announced that it had placed Fannie Mae and Freddie Mac under conservatorship because of their deteriorating financial positions and the "critical importance" that each company has to the continued functioning of the residential financial markets.[33]

FHFA has said that continuing audits of the GSEs determined that their financial positions were weaker than previously thought and that the GSEs were unlikely to survive without conservatorship. FHFA cited previous public statements that the GSEs needed to increase their capital and needed to strengthen management controls over operations.

What Was Fannie Mae's and Freddie Mac's Financial Position?

In placing the GSEs under conservatorship, their new regulator, FHFA, has said that they need assistance to survive. FHFA reported that changes in the economy and the GSEs' slow recovery from their earlier accounting and financial problems reduced their financial strength.[34]

The Office of Federal Housing Enterprise Oversight (OFHEO), which was Fannie Mae's and Freddie Mac's safety and soundness regulator before July 30, 2008, repeatedly said that the GSEs had adequate capital.[35] In other words, according to OFHEO, the GSEs had sufficient funds to survive their current financial difficulties.

This statement was difficult to verify independently. Details of the GSEs' portfolios and guarantees include confidential and proprietary information. In broad terms, the GSEs purchased slightly more than $169 billion of private label subprime MBSs in 2006 and 2007; they purchased slightly less than $58 billion of Alt-A MBSs in the same time period out of combined total mortgage purchases of $1.677 trillion.[36] At the end of 2007, the subprime and Alt-A MBSs represented 13.5% of the GSEs' total assets.

Why Did Fannie Mae's and Freddie Mac's Stock Prices Decline in 2008?

Changes in the perception of the risks that Fannie Mae and Freddie Mac face—in terms of future profitability and even continued financial viability—reduced the price that investors are willing to pay for a share of the enterprises. There was also concern that intervention by the federal government would reduce the value of the common stock.

Between the end of 2007 and August 1, 2008, Fannie's stock lost 72% of its value, while Freddie's fell by 77%. Between the end of 2007 and September 30, 2008, Fannie Mae's market capitalization fell from $38.8 billion to $825 million, and Freddie Mac's capitalization declined from $26.8 billion to $473 million.[37] As part of the Treasury's financial aid package of September 7, 2008, the GSEs agreed to issue warrants to the Treasury worth 79.9% of their outstanding stock. If Treasury were to exercise the warrants, current stockholders would own 20% of each enterprise instead of 100%. This is one explanation why the GSEs' stock prices declined further since September 7, 2008.

Fannie Mae and Freddie Mac are GSEs whose charters limit them to buying single family and multifamily home mortgages originated by others. This lack of diversification makes them more exposed to housing and mortgage market problems than other financial institutions such as commercial banks that have other lines of business. The GSEs' charters give them a special relationship with the federal government, sometimes called an implicit guarantee, which has allowed them to borrow at interest rates only slightly above those paid by the federal government. In conservatorship, the GSEs have an even closer connection with the government.

The two GSEs were very highly leveraged versions of banks: they borrow money to purchase mortgages, and they maximize profits by keeping their capital reserves close to the minimum required by their regulators. Like banks, the GSEs are required by law and by their regulators to maintain a certain ratio between their loans and reserves to protect against loan losses. A key component of reserves is shareholders' equity or the current value of the shareholders' investments. Using funds for capital provides safety, but it is less profitable in normal times than purchasing additional mortgages.

Why Did FHFA Act on September 7, 2008, Instead of Earlier or Later?

FHFA, in general, followed the same approach that the Federal Deposit Insurance Corporation uses when it places a bank in conservatorship: a series of requests for changes to the corporation and increased capital followed by the sudden takeover. Providing a deadline could provide the regulated entity with an incentive to take risky gambles in a last attempt to avoid being seized by the government. The FDIC usually seizes a bank by suddenly showing up on a Friday afternoon, closing the bank, and locking the doors. This gives it time to make necessary changes over the weekend and resume business operations on the next business day.

According to media reports, some large foreign investors had been reducing their holdings of GSE debt, MBSs, and stock.[38] This would have made it more difficult for the GSEs to borrow money to finance their portfolios going forward. For example, Bank of China, Ltd. is reported to have sold or not replaced maturing $4.6 billion of GSE debt, which reduced its GSE debt holdings to $17.3 billion as of June 30, 2008. These same media reported that Treasury officials contacted foreign central banks and others to reassure them of the creditworthiness of GSE debt.

FHFA worked with Treasury, the Fed, and the GSEs over the weekend of September 6 and 7, 2008. OFHEO and FHFA continue to take administrative actions to transfer authority and resources to FHFA. For example, on September 4, 2008, FHFA announced that it was publishing a legal notice of its existence in the *Federal Register*.[39]

Are There Precedents for Placing Fannie Mae and Freddie Mac under Conservatorship?

This is the first time that a GSE has been placed under conservatorship. It appears to also be the first time that the federal government has made a continuing commitment to a company (other than government corporations). On a more general level, the federal government has intervened in the past to assist many companies.[40] Since placing Fannie Mae and Freddie Mac under conservatorship, the federal government has intervened to support numerous companies, including General Motors, Chrysler, AIG, and various banks.[41]

Who Heads FHFA?

On August 6, 2009, FHFA Director James B. Lockhart announced that he would resign in the near future. President Obama named Senior Deputy Director for Housing Mission and Goals Edward J. DeMarco as acting director. President Obama has announced that he intends to nominate Joseph A. Smith, North Carolina Commissioner of Banks, to be the FHFA director.[42] The nomination requires Senate confirmation.

What Has Congress Done Previously to Improve the Financial Condition of the GSEs?

Congress has previously assisted GSEs that were in financial difficulty. When Fannie Mae was losing significant amounts of money in 1982, Congress passed the Miscellaneous Revenue Act of 1982 that provided tax benefits for Fannie Mae.[43] The Farm Credit System, another GSE, was aided with the Agricultural Credit Act of 1987, which authorized the issuance of $4 billion in bonds to support system members.[44]

Section 1117 of the Housing and Economic Recovery Act of 2008 (HERA) authorizes the Treasury to purchase any amount of GSE securities—debt or equity—if necessary to provide stability to financial markets, prevent disruptions in the availability of mortgage credit, or protect the taxpayer.[45] This means that if either of the two GSEs becomes unable to raise funds in private markets, the federal government could simply purchase the debt securities that the firms were unable to sell elsewhere, or recapitalize either firm by purchasing stock, possibly becoming the majority shareholder. The authority to enter into new support contracts expired on December 31, 2009.

This action sent a signal to the markets that the Treasury was prepared to intervene rather than let either GSE fail.

What Other Actions Has the Federal Government Taken to Address the Financial Condition of the GSEs?

On July 15, 2008, the Securities and Exchange Commission (SEC) issued an emergency order restricting short selling in the stock of 19 financial institutions, including Fannie and Freddie.[46] The SEC acted to prevent the possibility that false rumors could drive share prices down and cause the market to lose confidence, thereby cutting off the firms' access to credit markets, as happened to Bear Stearns in March 2008. The order restricting short sales of Fannie Mae and Freddie Mac stock was renewed on July 29, 2008, and expired on August 12, 2008, at 11:59 pm.

The government has also taken steps to prepare for possible future support for the GSEs. On July 13, 2008, the Federal Reserve Board of Governors granted the New York Fed the authority to lend directly to the GSEs.[47] Section 1118 of HERA requires the new GSE regulator to consult with the Fed to ensure financial market stability.

In addition to the Fed's existing general authority to be a lender of last resort, the GSEs' charters give the GSEs a special relationship to the nation's central bank.[48] The Fed can use the GSEs' bonds purchased on the secondary market for open market operations.[49] This could indirectly help the GSEs by adding to the demand for their debt and increasing its liquidity. The Fed announced that it would conduct a special program to purchase GSE debt and MBS in calendar 2009 and the first quarter of 2010.[50] Under this program, the Fed purchased more than $1 trillion of GSE debt and GSE-issued MBS.

Who Has Invested in the GSEs?

There is little information available about who holds GSE stock, bonds, and MBSs. The Fed reports statistics for combined ownership of government agency and GSE debt and GSE MBSs. At the end of the first half of 2010, non-U.S. investors held $1.213 trillion of $7.716 trillion agency and GSE securities.[51] Other large investors were U.S. commercial banks ($1.2 trillion), life insurance companies ($359 billion), state and local government retirement funds ($300 billion), mutual funds ($721 billion), asset-backed securities issuers ($97 billion), and the GSEs themselves ($388 billion).

Fannie Mae reports that central bank ownership of certain types of debt declined from 41.1% at the end of 2008 to 32.3% as of November 9, 2010.[52] Freddie Mac showed central bank ownership of its debt declined from slightly less than 40% at the end of 2008 to 24% as of September 30, 2010.[53]

What Recent Legislation Has Affected the GSEs?

Since the 110th Congress, there have been three bills signed into law that have had significant impacts on Fannie Mae, Freddie Mac, and the Federal Home Loan Banks. In chronological sequence, these are the Economic Stimulus Act of 2008, the Housing and Economic Recovery Act of 2008, and the American Recovery and Reinvestment Act of 2009. **Table 5**, below, summarizes these laws.

Table 5. Public Laws Affecting GSEs (Passed in 110th and 111th Congresses).

Bill Number	Title	P.L. Number	Date Enacted	Summary
H.R. 5140	Economic Stimulus Act of 2008 (ESA)	P.L. 110-185	February 13, 2008	Increased conforming loan limits in high-cost areas for mortgages originated between July 1, 2007 and December 31, 2008.
H.R. 3221	Housing and Economic Recovery Act of 2008 (HERA)	P.L. 110-289	July 30, 2008	Created Federal Housing Finance Agency to replace Office of Federal Housing Enterprise Oversight as combined GSE regulator.
H.R. 1	American Recovery and Reinvestment Act of 2009 (ARRA)	P.L. 111-5	February 7, 2009	Extended 2008 high-cost conforming loan limits to 2009 mortgages.
H.R. 3081	Continuing Appropriations Act of 2011	P.L. 111-242	September 30, 2010	Extended 2008 high-cost conforming loan limits for FY2011.

Source: The Congressional Research Service.

GLOSSARY

Alt-A mortgage	Either a mortgage made to a borrower with a credit history between prime and subprime, or a mortgage made to a prime borrower with less than traditional documentation.
ARRA	American Recovery and Reinvestment Act of 2009, P.L. 111-5.
ESA	Economic Stimulus Act of 2008, P.L. 110-185
FHFA	Federal Housing Finance Agency. Regulator of housing GSEs for mission, safety and soundness. Created by merger of existing government agencies, including OFHEO and HUD staff (who formerly had mission regulatory authority).
GSE	Government-sponsored enterprise.
GSECF	Government-sponsored enterprise credit facility. The Treasury's program to lend money to Fannie Mae, Freddie Mac, and the Federal Home Loan Banks using MBS as collateral. This program expired December 31, 2009, and was authorized by HERA.
HERA	Housing and Economic Recovery Act of 2008, P.L. 110-289.
MBSs	Mortgage-backed securities. A pool of mortgages sold to institutional investors.
OFHEO	Office of Federal Housing Enterprise. Safety and soundness regulator for Fannie Mae and Freddie Mac. Merged into Federal Housing Finance Agency.
prime mortgage	A mortgage made to a borrower with excellent credit history.
private-label MBSs	Mortgage-backed securities underwritten and sold by commercial and investment banks. They are not created by the GSEs or a government agency.
senior preferred stock	This stock is senior to (has priority over) all other common and preferred stock; it is the only stock currently receiving dividends.
subprime mortgage	A mortgage made to a borrower with a blemished credit history.

End Notes

[1] Office of Federal Housing Enterprise Oversight, *Report to Congress: 2008*, pp. 82 and 99, available at http://www.fhfa.gov/webfiles/2097/OFHEOReporttoCongress2008.pdf.

[2] FHFA, p. 116.

[3] FHFA, p. 133.

[4] OFHEO, p. 120. Regulatory capital is based on the amount of mortgages that a GSE has purchased. Risk-based capital is based on the riskiness of the mortgages a GSE has purchased. A GSE must have enough capital to meet the greater of these two amounts.

[5] Federal Housing Finance Agency, *Report to Congress 2008*, pp. 121 and 138, available at http://www.fhfa.gov/webfiles/2331/FHFAReportToCongress2008final.pdf. This reports on the GSEs (including the Federal Home Loan Banks) for 2008. The OFHEO report with the same title was issued in 2008 and covered the GSEs in 2007.

[6] U.S. Federal Housing Finance Agency, "Data as of November 9, 2010 on Treasury and Federal Reserve Purchase Programs for GSE and Mortgage-Related Securities," http://www.fhfa.gov/webfiles/19475/TreasFED11052010.pdf.

[7] U.S. Federal Housing Finance Agency, *Report to Congress: 2009*, pages 130 and 147, available at http://www.fhfa.gov/webfiles/15784/FHFAReportToCongress52510.pdf.

[8] U.S. Federal Housing Finance Agency, "Statement of FHFA Acting Director Edward J. DeMarco Concerning the Possible Transfer of Fannie Mae Low-Income Housing Tax Credits to Investors," press release, November 5, 2009, http://www.fhfa.gov/webfiles/15169/LIHTC%20 statement%2011%205%2009%20final.pdf.

[9] Federal National Mortgage Association, *Securities and Exchange Commission Form 8-K*, November 6, 2009, available at http://edgar.sec.gov/Archives/edgar/data/310522/ 000129993309004466/htm_35059.htm.

[10] U.S. Federal Housing Finance Agency, "2010–2011 Enterprise Housing Goals; Enterprise Book-entry Procedures," 75 Federal Register 55892-55939, September 14, 2010.

[11] U.S. Federal Housing Finance Agency, p 55936.

[12] U.S. Federal Housing Finance Agency, "2009 Enterprise Transition Affordable Housing Goals," 74 *Federal Register* 39873-39900, August 10, 2009.

[13] Stephen Labaton, "Offices Go Vacant at Fannie Mae and Freddie Mac," *New York Times*, April 15, 2009, Section B, p. 4.

[14] Federal National Mortgage Association, "Form 8-K," December 22, 2009, available at http://www.sec.gov/Archives/ edgar/data/310522/000095012309073307/w76668e8vk.htm, and Federal Home Loan Mortgage Corporation, "Form 8- K," December 22, 2009, available at http://sec.gov/Archives/edgar/data/1026214/000095012309073308/ f71239e8vk.htm. See, also, Federal Housing Finance Agency, "Fannie Mae, Freddie Mac Executive Compensation Significantly Reduced from Pre-Conservatorship Levels," press release, December 24, http://www.fhfa.gov/webfiles/ 15332/Exec_Comp_12_24_09.pdf.

[15] Representative Barney Frank, "Frank Calls on Lockhart to Cancel Fannie and Freddie Bonuses," press release, March 20, 2009, available at http://www.house.gov/apps/list/press/financialsvcs_dem/press032009.shtml, and Letter from James B. Lockhart, FHFA director, to Representative Barney Frank, March 20, 2009, available at http://www.fhfa.gov/webfiles/1670/32009ResponseLetter.pdf.

[16] *The 2008 Mortgage Market Statistical Annual*, Volume II (Bethesda, MD: Inside Mortgage Finance Publications, 2008), pp. 3, 9 and *The 2009 Mortgage Market Statistical Annual*, Volume II (Bethesda, MD: Inside Mortgage Finance Publications, 2009), pp. 3, 9. A

conforming mortgage is one that is under the conforming loan limit, which is as high as $729,750 in high-cost areas.

[17] P.L. 110-185, 122 Stat. 613 et seq.

[18] FHFA, pp. 30-36 and 46-51.

[19] A derivative is a financial contract whose value is linked to another financial instrument, price, or variable. For example, two companies could trade a derivative whose value was linked to the difference in the interest rates on 2- year and 10-year Treasury bonds.

[20] U.S. Treasury, "Treasury Issues Update on Status of Support for Housing Programs," December 24, 2009, available at http://www.treas.gov/press/releases/ 20091224153459245 43.htm.

[21] P.L. 111-5, Sec. 1117.

[22] U.S. Treasury, "Fact Sheet: GSE Mortgage Backed Securities Purchase Program," September 9, 2008, available at http://www.treas.gov/press/releases/reports/ mbs_factsheet_ 090708hp1128.pdf.

[23] Federal Reserve Bank of New York, *FAQs: MBS Purchase Program*, March 24, 2009, available at http://www.newyorkfed.org/markets/mbs_FAQ.HTML.

[24] U.S. Treasury, "Fact Sheet: Government Sponsored Enterprise Credit Facility," September 7, 2008, available at http://www.treas.gov/press/releases/reports/gsecf_factsheet_090708.pdf.

[25] U.S. Federal Housing Finance Agency, "FHFA Releases Projections Showing Range of Potential Draws for Fannie Mae and Freddie Mac," press release, October 21, 2010, http://www.fhfa.gov/webfiles/19409/Projections_102110.pdf.

[26] Letter from Douglas W. Elmendorf, Congressional Budget Office Director, to Barney Frank, Chairman, House Committee on Financial Services, September 16, 2010, http://www.cbo.gov/ftpdocs/117xx/doc11745/09-16-FrankLetter.pdf.

[27] Daniel E Teclaw and Vandana Sharma, *U.S. Government Cost To Resolve And Relaunch Fannie Mae And Freddie Mac Could Approach $700 Billion*, Standard & Poor's, November 4, 2010, p. 1, http://www2.standardandpoors.com/ spf/pdf/ events/ FITcon11410Article4.pdf.

[28] CRS Report RL34657, *Financial Institution Insolvency: Federal Authority over Fannie Mae, Freddie Mac, and Depository Institutions*, by David H. Carpenter and M. Maureen Murphy contains more information on this subject.

[29] See FHFA, pp. 21-52 for details on changes at Fannie Mae and Freddie Mac.

[30] Henry M. Paulson, Jr., Secretary of the Treasury, "Remarks by Secretary Henry M. Paulson, Jr. on Recommendations from the President's Working Group on Financial Markets," press release, March 13, 2008, available at http://www.ustreas.gov/press/releases/hp872.htm.

[31] Freddie Mac, *Form 10-K for the Fiscal Year Ending December 31*, p. 19, available at http://www.freddiemac.com/ investors/er/pdf/10k_031109.pdf, and Fannie Mae, Form *10-K for the Fiscal Year Ending December 31, 2008*, p. 9, available at http://www.fanniemae.com/ir/pdf/earnings

[32] P.L. 110-289, 122 Stat. 2654 et seq.

[33] Federal Housing Finance Agency, *Statement of FHFA Director James B. Lockhart*, September 9, 2008, available at http://www.ofheo.gov/newsroom.aspx? ID= 456&q1=1&q2=None.

[34] FHFA, *Statement of FHFA Director James B. Lockhart*, September 9, 2008. Available at http://www.ofheo.gov/newsroom.aspx?ID=456&q1=1&q2=None.

[35] OFHEO, Statement of OFHEO Director James B. Lockhart, July 10, 2008, available at http://www.ofheo.gov/ newsroom.aspx?ID=440&q1=1&q2=None.

[36] OFHEO, p. 113 and 116. Subprime and Alt-A MBS purchases prior to 2006 are not available.

[37] FHFA, pp. 121 and 138.

[38] Deborah Solomon, Michael Corkery, and Liz Rappaport, "Mortgage Bailout Is Greeted With Relief, Fresh Questions," *Wall Street Journal*, September 9, 2008, p. A1.

[39] U.S. Federal Housing Finance Agency, "Establishment of a New Independent Agency," 73 *Federal Register* 52356, September 9, 2008.

[40] CRS Report RL34423, *Government Interventions in Financial Markets: Economic and Historic Analysis of Subprime Mortgage Options*, by N. Eric Weiss discusses some of these actions.

[41] CRS Report RS22956, *The Cost of Government Financial Interventions, Past and Present*, by Baird Webel, Marc Labonte, and N. Eric Weiss.

[42] Office of the Press Secretary, The White House, "President Obama Announces More Key Administration Posts," press release, November 12, 2010, http://www.whitehouse.gov/the-press-office/2010/11/12/president-

[43] P.L. 97-362, 96 Stat. 1726 et seq.

[44] P.L. 100-233, 101 Stat. 1568 et seq.

[45] H.R. 3221, P.L. 110-289, 122 Stat. 2654 et seq.

[46] http://www.sec.gov/rules

[47] Federal Reserve Board of Governors, "Press Release," July 13, 2008, available at http://www.federalreserve.gov/ newsevents/press/other/20080713a.htm.

[48] The Fed's lender of last resort authority is delineated at 12 U.S.C. 343. Fannie Mae's charter is at 12 U.S.C. 1716b et seq., and Freddie Mac's charter is at 12 U.S.C. 1401.

[49] 12 U.S.C. 347c.

[50] Federal Reserve Bank of New York, "FAQs: MBS Purchase Program," August 20, 2010, available at http://www.ny.frb.org/markets/mbs_faq.html.

[51] Federal Reserve, "Agency- and GSE-backed Securities," *Flow of Funds Accounts of the United States*, September 2009, Table L. 210, available at http://www.federalreserve.gov/releases/z1/.

[52] Fannie Mae, "Noncallable Benchmark Notes Distribution Reports," *Benchmark Securities*, available at http://www.fanniemae.com/markets/debt/benchmark_securities/ general_ info/benchmark_notes_dist_reports.jhtml.

[53] Freddie Mac, *Freddie Mac Update*, October 2010, available at http://www.freddiemac.com/ investors/pdffiles/investor-presentation.pdf.

Housing Finance Reform in America
Editors: B. W. Virtanen, E. A. Laine
ISBN: 978-1-61324-350-3

Chapter 3

OPTIONS TO RESTRUCTURE FANNIE MAE AND FREDDIE MAC*

N. Eric Weiss

SUMMARY

This report analyzes some options that Congress might wish to consider for the future of Fannie Mae and Freddie Mac, which are federally chartered, stockholder-owned corporations known as government-sponsored enterprises or GSEs.

As GSEs, Fannie Mae and Freddie Mac have special privileges and obligations. Their charters give them a close relationship to the federal government that was widely (but not universally) viewed as an implicit federal guarantee of their bonds and mortgage-backed securities (MBS). The Housing and Economic Recovery Act of 2008 (HERA, P.L. 110-289) authorizes the Secretary of the Treasury to purchase unlimited amounts of obligations and other securities from the GSEs.

On September 7, 2008, the GSEs agreed to allow the Federal Housing Finance Agency to take over management of the GSEs by placing them under conservatorship. While under conservatorship, the GSEs have assumed a leading role in efforts to resolve and prevent foreclosure. As of the middle of 2009, the Treasury and the Federal Reserve had purchased $833.3 billion of MBS, $82.8 billion of debt, and $92 billion of senior preferred stock from Fannie Mae and Freddie Mac.

---

* This is an edited, reformatted and augmented version of a Congressional Research Services publication, dated September 17, 2009.

The options analyzed in this report include returning Fannie Mae and Freddie Mac to stockholder control as GSEs, merging them into the federal government as part of a government agency (sometimes called nationalization), and privatizing them. In addition, this report examines co-op insurance, a utility regulation model, government reinsurance, and the role of private bonds in home finance markets.

In addition to considering the future of Fannie Mae and Freddie Mac, Congress might wish to consider the future of the third housing GSE, the Federal Home Loan Bank System.

INTRODUCTION

This report analyzes options that Congress might wish to consider for the future of Federal National Mortgage Association and the Federal Home Loan Mortgage Corporation (commonly called Fannie Mae and Freddie Mac, respectively), which are federally chartered, stockholder-owned corporations known as government-sponsored enterprises or GSEs.[1] The GSEs' charters give them special benefits (such as exemption from certain securities laws and exemption from state and local income tax) and impose special obligations to support housing. In addition, prior to the GSEs going into conservatorship in 2008, the federal government was widely (but not universally) viewed as implicitly guaranteeing GSE bonds and mortgage-backed securities (MBS).

The GSEs were chartered by Congress with five purposes:

1) To stabilize the secondary mortgage market for residential mortgages;
2) To respond "appropriately" to the capital market;
3) To increase the liquidity of mortgages (including mortgages for low- and moderate-income families);
4) To promote access to mortgage credit in all areas of the nation (including underserved areas); and
5) To "manage and liquidate federally owned mortgage portfolios in an orderly manner, with a minimum of adverse effect upon the residential mortgage market and minimum loss to the Federal Government."[2]

It could be argued that between the time Fannie Mae and Freddie Mac became GSEs and the time that they were placed in conservatorship, they accomplished these goals except, perhaps, for operating with minimum loss to the federal government. Even under conservatorship, they continued (with assistance from the federal government) to fulfill their mission, although it can again be contested that they have operated with minimal loss to the federal government.

The Housing and Economic Recovery Act of 2008 (HERA, P.L. 110-289) authorized greater standby government support for the GSEs, including the FHLBanks, by allowing the Secretary of the Treasury to purchase unlimited amounts of obligations and other securities from the GSEs. The HERA-enhanced authority of the U.S. Department of the Treasury (Treasury) to assist the GSEs expires December 31, 2009. HERA created a new independent agency, the Federal Housing Finance Agency (FHFA), to regulate the GSEs.

On September 7, 2008, FHFA and the GSEs agreed to voluntary conservatorship, in which FHFA assumed control of Fannie Mae and Freddie Mac. Each GSE sold to Treasury $1 billion of senior preferred stock and gave Treasury warrants to purchase 79.9% of its common stock.[3] Treasury agreed to purchase a maximum of $100 billion (later raised to $200 billion) additional senior preferred stock to maintain a positive net worth of each GSE paying a 10% cash dividend, to purchase MBS from the GSEs, and to lend funds to the GSEs (including the FHLBanks).[4] In addition, the Federal Reserve has extended financial assistance to the GSEs in the form of MBS and debt purchases.[5] Conservatorship will end when the GSEs return to a safe and solvent condition.[6]

As of August 20, 2009, FHFA reported that the Treasury and the Federal Reserve had purchased $876.5 billion of MBS, $86.4 billion of debt, and $95.6 billion of senior preferred stock from Fannie Mae and Freddie Mac.[7] **Table 1** details this support.

Table 1. Government Financial Support for Fannie Mae and Freddie Mac ($ in billions).

Government Action	Fannie Mae	Freddie Mac	Total
Treasury Purchases of Senior Preferred Stock	44.9	50.7	95.6
Treasury Purchases of MBS	89.0	82.8	171.8
Federal Reserve Purchases of MBS	445.3	259.4	704.7
Federal Reserve Purchase of GSE Debt	45.1	41.3	86.4
Total Government Support	624.3	434.2	1058.5

Source: Federal Housing Finance Agency, *Current Data on Treasury and Federal Reserve Purchase Programs for GSE and Mortgage-Related Securities*, August 20, 2009, http://www.fhfa.gov/webfiles/14778/TSYFed082009.pdf.

This report discusses alternatives available to Congress for restructuring Fannie Mae and Freddie Mac; the list is not exhaustive—it probably is impossible to develop a complete list. The options take as a starting point that Fannie Mae and Freddie Mac return to financial health and are able to leave their current conservatorship. This might not occur. In 2008, Fannie Mae lost $58.7 billion, and Freddie Mac lost $50.2 billion. To maintain positive net worth, Fannie Mae has sold $44.9 billion of preferred stock to the Treasury, and Freddie Mac has sold $50.7 billion. If Fannie Mae or Freddie Mac were to fail, they would be placed in receivership and their assets sold to satisfy their creditors.

HERA requires that a GSE be placed in mandatory receivership and its assets liquidated if (1) the GSE's assets have been less than its liabilities for 60 consecutive days, or (2) the GSE has not been paying its bills (except for debts subject to bona fide dispute) for the past 60 days.[8]

In debating alternatives for the futures of Fannie Mae and Freddie Mac, Congress might wish to consider whether the five goals are still germane. For example, the Riegle-Neal Interstate Banking and Branching Efficiency Act of 1994 (P.L. 103-328) may have made the fourth point in the GSEs' charters (promoting mortgage credit throughout the nation) unnecessary because the act allowed interstate banking and led to more equal access to call credit throughout the nation.

Fannie Mae's and Freddie Mac's Business Models

Fannie Mae's and Freddie Mac's business models have evolved similarly. They both

- purchase single-family mortgages that other companies have originated;[9]
- guarantee that the mortgages will be paid and pool the mortgages to create MBS;
- sell the MBS to institutional investors, or keep them in their own investment portfolios. If the GSE decides to keep the MBS, it borrows money by selling bonds to finance the MBS.

For many years, the GSEs were very profitable using this business model because they were widely viewed as having a close relationship to the federal government. Some called it an implicit guarantee. This allowed the GSEs to guarantee their MBS and to finance their investment portfolios at lower cost than competitors, which had neither GSE charters nor a special relationship with the federal government. GSE profitability was increased by their charter provisions such as those exempting them from state and local income taxes, and by lower capital requirements than their non-GSE competitors. To enhance profits, the GSEs used a variety of techniques, some of which increased the riskiness of the GSEs' finances:

- Because short-term interest rates are normally lower than longer-term interest rates, the GSEs financed their investment portfolios of MBS by borrowing for short periods of time. This strategy could reduce GSE profits if interest rates were higher when this debt was refinanced.[10] The GSEs reduced their vulnerability to increased interest rates by the use of financial derivatives.
- Having nationwide geographic diversification reduced the GSEs' credit or default risk. Regional declines in home prices—such as the home price decline of approximately 25% between 1985 and 1990 in the "Oil Patch"—were balanced by stable prices in other areas. The GSEs further reduced their risk by purchasing insurance from financial guaranty insurance companies.
- The GSEs found creative ways to satisfy the requirement in their charters that mortgages for more than 80% of the value of a house have credit enhancements such as mortgage insurance. For example, one GSE would purchase the first mortgage for 80% of a home's value, and the other GSE would purchase a second mortgage for 5% or even 15% of the same home's value. This resulted in larger mortgages and more fees for the GSEs, but increased the severity of losses when default occurred.
- Tax planning techniques, including purchasing tax-exempt bonds and low-income housing tax credits (LIHTCs), reduced taxes. The risk of these strategies was that if the GSEs' earnings decreased more than anticipated, the tax planning expenditures would not be usable and could increase losses.
- Compared with many other types of financial institutions, the GSEs were required to keep less capital as a reserve against possible losses. This increased leverage made possible higher profits, but increased the risk of larger losses compared to holding more capital.

GSE FINANCIAL STATUS

For the second quarter of 2009, Fannie Mae reported its eighth straight quarter of losses, whereas Freddie Mac reported a profit for the first time in eight quarters. Since the third quarter of 2007, Fannie Mae has reported total losses of $102 billion, and Freddie Mac has had a net loss of $63 billion. To maintain a positive net worth, Fannie Mae and Freddie Mac have sold to Treasury senior preferred stock in the amounts of $46 billion, and $52 billion, respectively. In short, if not for the provisions of HERA, both Fannie Mae and Freddie Mac would be insolvent. Prior to HERA, there were no provisions for the GSEs to enter receivership and hence no procedures available to liquidate their assets.[11]

The GSEs' main assets are the mortgages that they have in their investment portfolios. According to their monthly volume summaries at the end of 2008, Fannie Mae had a gross mortgage portfolio of $787 billion and other investments of $83 billion for a total of $870 billion in assets compared with debt of $884 billion. Freddie Mac had a mortgage portfolio of $805 billion and other investments of $64 billion for a total of $869 billion in assets compared with debt of $870 billion.

Alternatives to Liquidation

If FHFA's conservatorship is not able to return the GSEs to financial health, there are at least two approaches that could avoid complete liquidation of the GSEs.

"Bad Bank" Option

First, the "bad bank" approach would mirror one technique used by the Federal Deposit Insurance Corporation (FDIC) to resolve insolvent banks.[12] The FDIC creates a "bad bank" to hold the problem assets, leaving the good assets with the original bank. Without the problem assets, the original bank is financially viable and possibly able to attract new capital. In the case of the GSEs, delinquent mortgages and MBS, with related guarantees, would be transferred to the new entity. The bad bank would need capital to purchase the nonperforming assets from the GSEs. Because the private sector would be unlikely to invest in the bad bank, the capital to purchase the assets would probably come from the federal government. Timing the creation of this new entity could be important to ensure that the GSEs do not become insolvent again.

The bad bank could require continuing funds from the government, but might continue in operation in the hope that as housing and financial markets recover, the value of the mortgages and MBS would increase to exceed the value of the guarantees.

Restructuring Senior Preferred Stock

Second, the GSEs' senior preferred stock could be restructured so that the 10% dividends were less of a financial burden to the GSEs. This could save the GSEs $8billion to $9 billion annually, but would reduce the federal government's income by the same amount. The federal government could accomplish this by writing off some or all of the cost of the senior preferred stock or by agreeing to accept a lower annual dividend.

The advantage of restructuring the senior preferred stock is that it would allow the GSEs to return to stockholder control, which is discussed in detail below. The disadvantage is that the GSEs and their stockholders would have received significant financial benefits without fully having paid for those benefits. This could lead to the expectation of future government support and encourage the GSEs to assume more risk than they would without this expectation.

Receivership

HERA provides for voluntary and involuntary receivership. FHFA is required to place a GSE in involuntary receivership if either the GSE's liabilities exceed its assets for 60 days, or if a GSE fails to pay its bills (except for those being disputed) for 60 days. FHFA is authorized by HERA to create a temporary successor.

RESTRUCTURING OPTIONS

Assuming that one way or another both GSEs return to financial solvency, some of the options that Congress might consider are:

- return Fannie Mae and Freddie Mac to their stockholders with little or no change to their congressional charters;
- eliminate their GSE status and convert Fannie Mae and Freddie Mac into private corporations;
- eliminate their GSE status and convert Fannie Mae and Freddie Mac into a government agency; or
- make supplementary changes to support the secondary mortgage market, such as providing government reinsurance of MBS or encouraging the use of covered bonds.

Table 2 summarizes the options.

Table 2. Summary of GSE Restructuring Options.

Category	Option	Summary
Maintaining GSE status	Return control to stockholders	Return GSEs to status prior to being placed in conservatorship with no changes to oversight
	Retain GSE status with additional regulation	Return GSEs to status prior to being placed in conservatorship with additional oversight
	Explicit guarantee	Federal government would explicitly guarantee MBS. (The explicit guarantee probably would eliminate the GSE status of Fannie Mae and Freddie Mac. See 2 U.S.C. 622(8))
	Utility model	Return GSEs to status prior to being placed in conservatorship, but regulate their profits
	Split GSEs	Return GSEs to status prior to being placed in conservatorship, but divide the two GSEs into many GSEs
	Combine with FHLBanks	Fannie Mae and Freddie Mac would be merged with the FHLBanks, which is the third housing GSE
Eliminate GSE status	Government agency	Merge the GSEs with FHA and Ginnie Mae, which are parts of HUD, or convert the GSEs into a new government agency
	Privatization	Remove all of the GSEs' special obligations and privileges by revoking their Congressional charters

Category	Option	Summary
	Privatization with Co-Op Insurance	Remove all of the GSEs' special obligations and privileges by revoking their Congressional charters, and organize a co-operative to provide first line insurance for MBS.
Supplementary	Reinsurance	Provide explicit federal backup insurance for MBS
	Covered bonds	Encourage the issuance of overcollaterized MBS

Source: CRS.

This report continues by discussing the advantages and disadvantages of these options and by adding more detail to the options.

Options Maintaining GSE Status

By law, the GSEs' conservatorship will end if they meet their minimum capital requirements, or when the FHFA director determines that ending conservatorship would be in the public interest. If this occurs, there are a number of options that could be considered that would include maintaining Fannie Mae and Freddie Mac as GSEs. These are returning control to the stockholders with no additional modification, imposing additional regulations on the GSEs, explicitly guaranteeing the GSEs' MBS, imposing utility-type profitability limits on the GSEs, merging Fannie Mae and Freddie Mac into the Federal Home Loan Bank System, and issuing additional GSE charters.

Option: Return Control to Stockholders

Congress could decide to make little or no change to the GSEs' charters. The GSEs would continue to be stockholder-owned companies with special charters and special obligations to support the housing market.

If this option were adopted, common stockholders would regain their right to elect the boards of directors, which in turn would appoint senior management. Dividends to preferred stockholders could resume. Dividends on the senior preferred stock owned by the federal government would continue. The GSEs would decide whether to retire the senior preferred stock held by the federal government. The boards of directors could resume common dividends. Bond payments would continue, and after December 31, 2009, the

GSEs would shrink their portfolios by 10% annually until their portfolios were less than $250 billion.[13]

Return to stockholder control implicitly assumes that the GSEs would return to profitability. Since entering into conservatorship, the GSEs have issued to Treasury approximately $95 billion in senior preferred stock. This stock pays an annual cash dividend of 10% or an annual preferred stock dividend of 12%. Since 1980, Fannie Mae's income has been sufficient to pay this cash dividend in only four years: 2005, 2004, 2003, and 2001; Freddie Mac could have done this only in 2002. Based on historical data, the GSEs are unlikely to be able to sustain the annual cash dividend payments. Unless the government were to agree to a reduction in the 10% dividend or the amount of senior preferred stock, it seems unlikely that GSEs would have value to common stockholders.

Moreover, in agreeing to conservatorship, the GSEs each gave the federal government warrants to purchase 79.9% of their common stock at $0.00001 per share. Before effective control could be returned to common stockholders, the GSEs probably would need to reach some agreement with the federal government over the disposition of these warrants. Based on similar past government intervention such as Chrysler in 1979 and Continental Illinois in 1985, alternative dispositions of these warrants include federal government exercise, sale of the warrants through a federal government open market auction of them (which the GSEs could win), and federal government cancellation of the warrants.[14] In mid-2009, with its stock trading at approximately $0.65, Fannie Mae had a market capitalization of slightly more than $700 million. This would make 80% of the enterprise worth $560 million. In mid-2009, Freddie Mac's stock price was $0.70 and its market capitalization was slightly more than $460 million, making 79.9% of Freddie Mac $368 million. Because the GSEs "have succession until dissolved by Act of Congress," it is not clear what limits there might be on an outside company purchasing the warrants.

Arguments in Favor

The argument in favor of the no change option is that by some measures the GSEs have been successes; since the GSEs became stockholder owned (1968 in the case of Fannie Mae, and 1989 in the case of Freddie Mac), only the recent exceptional housing markets have required government intervention.[15] Arguably, the GSEs have led to many changes in the nation's mortgage markets that have improved efficiency and consumer choice. Some might debate whether these innovations have been improvements and others might claim to have invented them before the GSEs:

- Standardizing mortgages, which has contributed to economies of scale and lower interest rates for homeowners;
- Automating and standardizing underwriting, which has reduced the cost of obtaining a home mortgage;
- Making widespread certain features such as assumable mortgages and mortgages without prepayment penalties, both of which facilitate refinancing;
- Tapping new sources of funding including pension funds, trusts, and international investors, which has led to lower mortgage interest rates;
- Eliminating state and local mortgage interest rate differentials, which has lowered mortgage rates in some parts of the nation, but possibly increased them in others;
- Innovating in affordable housing and equal housing opportunity, and
- Creating a liquid secondary mortgage market, which has lowered mortgage interest rates.

Arguments Against

There are at least three broad arguments against returning the GSEs to their former status. First, the GSEs' history includes previous financial and management problems. In 1982, Fannie Mae was in financial distress, and the government intervened after Congress passed the Miscellaneous Revenue Act of 1982, which provided some tax benefits for Fannie Mae.[16] In the early 2000s, Fannie Mae and Freddie Mac both had serious accounting and management issues that led to consent agreements with the Office of Federal Housing Enterprise Oversight (OFHEO), which then regulated them, and the Securities and Exchange Commission (SEC); and the GSEs' leaderships were replaced. Fannie Mae paid about $400 million in fines, and Freddie Mac paid $125 million in fines.

Second, many, if not all, of the changes used as points in favor of returning the GSEs to stockholder control arguably would have occurred without Fannie Mae and Freddie Mac, although possibly not as early. Other large mortgage market participants, such as banks and mortgage insurance companies, could have standardized and automated the lending process. Ginnie Mae, a government agency, issued the first MBS.

Prior to the Riegel-Neal Interstate Banking and Branching Efficiency Act of 1994 (P.L. 103-328), banks were not allowed to operate in more than one state. Banks in one state might have many deposits relative to the demand for loans, and reduce interest rates, including those on home mortgages, to encourage borrowing. At the same time, banks in another state might have relatively few deposits compared to loan demand and would increase interest rates. Because of the ban on interstate banking, money could not easily flow between states to equalize interest rates. One of the GSEs' roles was to move funds to where demand for home mortgages was greatest. After Riegel-Neal permitted interstate banking, it was arguably inevitable that interest rates and mortgage interest rates would become uniform across the nation.

Third, the conservatorship of the GSEs made several changes in the future financial environment of the GSEs.

- Having previously intervened, the federal government may be perceived as likely to provide any necessary future financial support to the GSEs to pay bonds, despite charter provisions that state that GSE debts are not guaranteed by the federal government.
- Attracting new common stockholders could be difficult because of the federal government's taking control and stopping dividend payments to common stockholders. The burden of the senior preferred dividends and the warrants could make it very difficult to raise additional capital by selling new stock.
- Attracting new preferred stockholders could be difficult since the federal government stopped dividend payments to preferred stockholders.

Option: Retain GSE Status with Additional Regulation

In returning the GSEs to stockholder control, additional statutory and regulatory oversight could be imposed. This could include increased minimum capital requirements, limits to executive compensation, limits to stockholder dividends, changed accounting procedures, or portfolio size limits. Regulations arguably could help prevent future financial problems with the GSEs. An argument can be made that if the government were to give the GSEs more explicit or implicit assistance, the GSEs might have to broaden their support of housing.[17]

On the one hand, an advantage of returning the GSEs to their stockholders while imposing additional regulation is that it is a return to a familiar model. The GSE support for affordable housing could continue.

On the other hand, making changes to GSE regulation has been a very contentious issue whenever Congress debated it in the past; previous GSE regulation failed to prevent their going into conservatorship; and the federal government has expended large amounts of money to maintain the GSEs' financial viability.

Option: Retain GSE Status with Explicit Guarantee

It can be argued that prior to 1992, the implicit guarantee in the GSEs' charters was provided at no cost to the GSEs. The Federal Housing Enterprises Financial Safety and Soundness Act of 1992 (FHEFSSA, P.L. 102-550) authorized HUD to set explicit affordable housing goals for the GSEs. The GSEs were not expected to lose money on mortgages purchased to meet the housing goals, but they were not guaranteed that the housing goals mortgages would be as profitable as other mortgages. Thus the implicit guarantee was provided at an implicit cost. One problem with implicit guarantees and implicit costs is that since their terms are not clearly defined, they are hard to value.

A possible solution to this concern would be for the government to make the guarantee explicit and to charge an explicit guarantee fee. The exact terms of the guarantee could be stated. Homebuyers might directly pay this guarantee fee as they now pay the FHA's guarantee fee, or the GSEs could be charged the guarantee fee. In the latter case, the GSEs could decide how much of the fee to pass on to borrowers. By changing the guarantee fee, the federal government could increase or decrease the GSEs' profits.

Instead of guaranteeing the GSEs, the federal government could make the explicit guarantee available on all mortgages that met certain standards. This would be similar in effect to enlarging the FHA's guarantee program to cover more of the mortgage market. The federally guaranteed mortgages could be bundled and securitized. Since they would have a federal guarantee, Ginnie Mae could securitize these mortgages.

One issue with this option would be deciding what types of mortgages could be guaranteed and how new types of mortgages could be added to the program. Guarantees for mortgages that would be originated anyway would be an expense to the GSEs and a contingent liability for the government that would not increase homeownership. If a lender were to develop an extremely risky new type of mortgage, should the government guarantee it? Should the government charge an actuarially sound guarantee fee? If so, would not the private sector offer the same guarantee?

Option: Retain GSE Status with Utility Model

In what is frequently called the utility model, the federal government could explicitly regulate the GSEs' profit margins much as state utility regulators control utility profits. The federal government could either explicitly approve new GSE products, or new GSE products could be implicitly regulated by setting guarantee rates.[18]

Some have suggested that only one federally chartered company would be eligible for the guarantee, but others have suggested that at least two GSEs would be eligible. Public utilities' regulation has been justified on the basis that there are economies of scale that can be captured if there is only one utility. By restricting competition, only one water main, telephone line, natural gas pipe, or electrical line needs to be constructed to connect each home and business with the utility. The regulator is charged with balancing the economic interests of consumers against those of the monopoly provider. For example, while Fannie Mae and Freddie Mac have found their retained portfolios of MBS to be profitable, the net value to homeowners is subject to much debate. In the utility model, the retained portfolios might be restricted to simplify regulatory oversight and to reduce risks.

It is debatable whether there are economies of scale that would result in savings if there were only one or two mortgage companies receiving federal guarantees.

Option: Split the GSEs

Arguably, one of the sources of the GSEs' problems has been that there are only two of them. Over time, Fannie Mae and Freddie Mac became virtual twins and essentially divided the conforming U.S. mortgage market between them.[19] The result was, it could be argued, not much different from having a monopolist GSE that could charge high prices and make persistently large profits in the absence of competition. Prior to the financial turmoil that started in 2007, there were dozens of non-GSEs in the relatively small private label MBS market. Some claim that the market would have supported more than two GSEs issuing MBS, if more GSE charters had been issued.

One option to increase competition would be to split the GSEs into many more. If each GSE were split into, say, 10 equal parts (for a total of 20 housing GSEs), each of the 20 resulting GSEs would have mortgage portfolios of one-tenth its parent and have one-tenth of its parent's mortgage guarantees outstanding.[20] Based on year end 2008 financial statements, the baby Fannie Maes would each have a mortgage portfolio and outstanding guarantees of $298 billion; the baby Freddie Macs would each have a mortgage portfolio and outstanding guarantees of $221 billion.

It might be that 20 identical GSEs would be under financial stress at the same time. One way to reduce the probability of this would be to split the GSEs in such a way that they were not all the same. To promote diversity among the new GSEs, they could be created with different geographic coverage, or to specialize in certain types of housing such as condominiums or multifamily rental housing. Existing stockholders would receive shares in the new GSEs. On the other hand, this specialization could leave new GSEs more vulnerable to declines affecting only certain types of housing.

The GSEs would continue to be regulated. One argument for creating many GSEs is that competition among the GSEs could supplement formal regulatory oversight.

Option: Incorporate Fannie Mae and Freddie Mac into Federal Home Loan Bank System

A slightly different option would be to incorporate the GSEs into the Federal Home Loan Bank (FHLBank) system. Each regional FHLBank is owned by its member banks; shares of the FHLBanks are not traded on a stock exchange. The 12 regional banks form a collective GSE that raises funds (called advances) that are lent to the members, who pledge mortgages and MBS as collateral. The debt is the joint and several liability of the individual FHLBanks; if one bank were to become insolvent, the other banks would remain responsible for its debts. Freddie Mac was created as part of the FHLBank system to sell its mortgages on the secondary market.

The FHLBank system could purchase Fannie Mae and Freddie Mac, which would become a mortgage securitization facility (or facilities) within the FHLBank system. The lenders that are members of the FHLBank system presently own the FHLBanks and would similarly own the GSEs.

Alternatively, Fannie Mae's and Freddie Mac's mortgage portfolios and other assets could be divided among the 12 FHLBanks. Some resources, such as mortgage securitization, could be merged into the FHLBanks' Office of Finance, which provides centralized financial services for the regional banks.

The advantage of this approach is that the FHLBank system has never—not even in the Depression—lost money on an advance. The counter argument is that history may not predict the future: FHLBank members are insured by the FDIC. In the event of a member failure, the FHLBank has the mortgages that the member pledged as collateral on its advances. If these are insufficient to meet the member's obligations to the FHLBank, the FHLBank can use its "super lien," which gives it a priority claim over other unsecured creditors. FDIC research suggests that the FHLBanks have no incentive to risk-adjust the interest rate on advances.[21] The FDIC argues that this encourages the FHLBanks to take excessive risks because the bank keeps the profit, but the FDIC gets the risk. In addition, in the event of a member failure, the FHLBank has priority ahead of the FDIC on assets.

Option: Issue Additional GSE Charters

Another option would be to issue new GSE charters. Congress could establish the requirements for obtaining these new charters and limit the activities that the new GSEs could undertake. The GSEs could, if Congress so desires, contribute to an insurance fund similar to the FDIC for banks. Either the existing GSE regulator, the FHFA, or a new regulator would oversee the GSEs. Since Fannie Mae and Freddie Mac would retain all of their current assets and liabilities, there arguably would be no need to compensate existing stockholders of Fannie Mae and Freddie Mac, but the stockholders might object to the new competition. The government could charge a fee for the GSE charters. Market competition among the many GSEs could supplement regulatory oversight.

Options Eliminating GSE Status

Fannie Mae and Freddie Mac are GSEs because of their charters, which were created by enactment of legislation, and legislative action could repeal the charters. In some circumstances, repeal might raise legal and other concerns about financial compensation for current common and preferred stockholders, assumption of responsibility for paying off existing bondholders, guarantees of timely payment of mortgages, and other liabilities. On the other hand, Treasury has warrants to purchase nearly 80% of each GSE's common stock at nominal cost making stockholder approval of a government proposal a certainty.

The GSEs could continue with state charters like other financial intermediaries including commercial banks. In the early 1990s, the Student Loan Marketing Association (Sallie Mae) sought to relinquish its GSE status because of the financial burdens that came with its being a GSE and to make loans that it could not as a GSE.[22] In 1996, Congress agreed to allow Sallie Mae to relinquish its congressional charter and give up its GSE status.[23] Sallie Mae became a stockholder-owned company with no special privileges in 2004.

If the GSE charters were repealed, Congress might wish to consider whether the GSEs' securitization of mortgages should be continued by a government agency. The GSEs have been able to compete against the government programs (FHA's mortgage insurance, the Veterans' Affairs mortgage guarantees, and the Department of Agriculture's rural housing programs) by creating a broader product than some government programs, and by competing on price.

Some research has suggested that the GSEs' biggest competitive advantage against other private sector mortgage lenders derived from the close relationship with the federal government which allowed the GSEs to borrow funds at lower rates compared to other mortgage lenders.[24] Without GSEs and their funding advantage, investment bankers might securitize conforming mortgages that were formerly securitized by the GSEs.

The impact of the GSEs on mortgage interest rates is much debated. The current spread between conforming and jumbo mortgages is greater than the historical average. A 2006 Federal Reserve study found that the GSEs did not reduce interest rates, but cites other studies that found interest rate reductions of 4 to 35 basis points with older studies finding greater reductions.[25] (One basis point is 0.01%.) This research suggests that there could be a small increase in mortgage interest rates if the GSEs were to cease securitizing mortgages.

In the current unusual financial environment, the GSEs, Ginnie Mae (which securitizes government-insured and guaranteed mortgages), and FHLBanks are by far the most active source of mortgage funds. However, the GSEs have been extremely dependent on selling their MBS to the Fed and Treasury. Without the Fed and Treasury, it is unlikely that the GSEs would be a significant source of mortgage funding.

Option: Government Agency

Another option would be to make the GSEs a government agency. Ginnie Mae, officially the Government National Mortgage Association, an office within the Department of Housing and Urban Development, purchases and securitizes government-insured and government-guaranteed mortgages in much the same way that the GSEs purchase and securitize conforming mortgages. Ginnie Mae contracts with investment banks on Wall Street to do the actual securitization of their mortgage purchases. This allows Ginnie Mae to function with approximately 60 employees yet be responsible for approximately $577 billion in Ginnie Mae MBS.

Ginnie Mae's contractor purchases government-insured and guaranteed mortgages and pools them into MBS. Ginnie Mae adds the federal government's guarantee that the MBS purchasers will be paid, and the contractor sells the MBS to institutional investors. Until it became stockholder owned in 1968, Fannie Mae was part of Ginnie Mae.

One issue that Congress might wish to examine is how to ensure adaptability of mortgage markets to meet changing conditions. The FHA's status as a government agency gives it limited flexibility to modify programs without legislative action.

On the one hand, this lack of adaptability has prevented FHA from responding to new market conditions, which has resulted in reduced market share. On the other hand, this has reflected Congress' will and FHA/Ginnie Mae did not guarantee or purchase subprime or Alt-A mortgages. At the end of the second quarter of 2009, 4.8% of FHA-backed mortgages were 90 or more days delinquent, compared to 3.67% of all mortgages.[26]

If Fannie Mae and Freddie Mac were to become a government agency, it is possible that many of the current staff and directors of the GSEs would find other employment. Potential reasons include duplication of functions, or because the salaries of current GSE employees would be reduced to fit the government pay schedule currently used at FHA and Ginnie Mae. Financial regulators, such as the Federal Reserve, FDIC, and Office of the Comptroller of the Currency, have the authority to use different pay schedules.

Option: Privatization

Fully privatized GSEs would no longer have special status from the federal government. They would be owned by investors. GSE stockholders would receive stock in the new companies. The stock of the new companies probably would trade on one or more stock exchanges. The new companies would assume the assets (retained portfolios) and liabilities (bonds, MBS and guarantees) of the existing GSEs.

At the end of 2008, GSE MBS represented 64% of the nation's MBS, an increase compared to previous years due, at least in part, the withdrawal of other securitizers.[27] Some might consider this to be too dominant, and Congress might consider dividing the GSEs into many companies as part of a privatization process. Congress might wish to consider if each of the new non-GSEs should be similar, or if some might specialize in geography or some other factor. This could reduce the probability that multiple mortgage lenders would simultaneously encounter financial difficulty, but would eliminate some of the risk reduction that comes from diversification.

Option: Privatization with Co-Op Insurance

A co-op to insure MBS could be included in the privatization option. This would be similar to a private Federal Home Loan Bank System and share some features with Lloyd's of London, which also uses a co-op insurance business model. The co-op would create MBS from mortgages purchased from members. Members would be required to buy stock in the co-op proportional to the volume of mortgages sold to the co-op, and part of the proceeds from the mortgage sales would be posted as collateral against losses. The collateral could be released as the mortgages age.

The co-op members stock could be sold if collateral were insufficient to cover losses. Beyond this, members would have no liability. The result would be that individual co-op members would keep their profits and share their losses.

The co-op would decide pricing, eligibility requirements, and credit requirements. The government would supervise the co-op for safety and soundness, and it would explicitly bear the risk of catastrophic disaster. In return, the government could charge the co-op a fee for supervision and risk.

If the co-op's rules allowed for wide membership, this option could encourage competition in mortgage securitization. Members would have a stake up to the amount of equity in the co-op, in the behavior of other members. A member who used the co-op to insure risky mortgages would be risking all of the members' equity and increasing the risk that the federal government's catastrophic insurance might have to be used.

Supplementary Options

There are at least two supplementary options that could operate independent of how the GSEs are restructured: government reinsurance and covered bonds.

Reinsurance

The government could provide catastrophic reinsurance to the secondary mortgage market. This would be similar to the reinsurance provided under the Terrorism Risk Insurance Act of 2002 (TRIA, P.L. 107-297). GSEs and others selling MBS in the secondary market would provide primary insurance to purchasers. The GSEs or others creating MBS experienced losses exceeding a certain limit, the federal government would provide insurance. This would allow many financial institutions to compete in the secondary mortgage market.

The terms of this insurance could be determined by statute or by regulation. Some of the factors to be considered would be: how large of a loss (dollars or percentage) would primary insurance incur before the reinsurance became effective? Who should be eligible for the reinsurance program? Would the reinsurance be 100%, or would these losses be shared? How should premiums be determined?

Covered Bonds

Covered bonds are a method of raising funds for mortgages that provides more security to purchasers than non-GSE MBS provide currently.[28] While the GSEs guarantee that the purchasers of their MBS will receive timely payment of principal and interest, the issuers of private label MBS do not include any such guarantee. If a mortgage borrower defaults, the losses flow to the private label MBS holder as specified in the MBS prospectus.

Covered bonds seek to reduce the risk of financial loss to the bond purchaser. Regular bonds are backed by the income of the issuer and have no specific collateral. Covered bonds have collateral and a claim on the income and assets of the issuer. Typically, covered bonds have more collateral than the value of the bonds. If the value of the collateral declines (due to prepayment, default, foreclosure, etc.), the issuer must add additional collateral. In a best practices paper, Treasury said that there should be at least an extra 5% collateral coverage, that only 30-year fixed-rate mortgages should be included, and that the maximum loan-to-value ratio on mortgages included should be 80%.[29]

Because covered bonds have a priority claim on the assets of the issuer, the remaining claimants are likely to receive less in bankruptcy or receivership. In the case of an insured depository institution such as a bank or thrift, covered bonds would increase the FDIC's losses. Presently, covered bonds may not exceed 4% of an FDIC-insured institution's liabilities.[30] This currently limits the ability of insured depository institutions to issue covered bonds. Some have proposed that covered mortgage bonds could be issued using MBS from the GSEs or their successors.

Covered bonds are popular in Europe where the covered bond issuer typically originates the mortgage, which some analysts believe aligns the interests of originators and bond holders. European covered bonds reportedly have not defaulted since at least 1899.

Covered bonds are attractive because they could reduce the risks to purchasers of private label MBS and increase competition in the secondary mortgage market.

Legislative Action

No legislation has been introduced in the 111[1th] Congress to reorganize Fannie Mae or Freddie Mac. On June 3, 2009, the Subcommittee on Capital Markets, Insurance, and Government Sponsored Enterprises of the House Financial Services Committee held a hearing, "The Present Condition and Future Status of Fannie Mae and Freddie Mac."

Unless extended by Congress, Treasury's authority to purchase GSE obligations and securities, including MBS and senior preferred stock, will expire on December 31, 2009. Essentially, Treasury can continue to purchase senior preferred stock (up to $200 billion for each GSE) after December 31, 2009, but it cannot exceed the $200 billion limits.[31] The Federal Reserve's authority to purchase MBS and debt does not expire.

The Obama Administration has released a report that lists six options for the future of the GSEs:

1) Privatization,
2) Gradual liquidation,

3) Merger with a government agency,
4) Public utility-type regulation of the GSEs,
5) Conversion to an insurance company, and
6) Dissolution of the GSEs into smaller companies.[32]

The Administration is to report to Congress on these options as part of the FY2011 budget process.

End Notes

[1] 2 U.S.C. 622(8) defines "government-sponsored enterprise." The Federal Home Loan Banks (FHLBanks) collectively are a third housing GSE. Following common practice, the report uses GSE to refer to Fannie Mae and Freddie Mac. If the FHLBanks are included, this will be explicitly stated.

[2] 12 U.S.C. 1716 (Fannie Mae), and 12 U.S.C. 1451 Note (Freddie Mac).

[3] A company's preferred stockholders do not elect the board of directors or otherwise exercise control over the firm, but payment of their specified dividend has a priority over the payment of dividends to common stockholders. A warrant is a type of option issued by a company to purchase stock at a specified price.

[4] The initial contracts to purchase a maximum of $100 billion from each GSE were amended May 6, 2009, to increase the maximum to $200 billion each. See CRS Report RL34427, *Financial Turmoil: Federal Reserve Policy Responses*, by Marc Labonte.

[5] Federal Reserve Bank of New York, "FAQs: MBS Purchase Program," press release, March 24, 2009, http://www.newyorkfed.org/markets/mbs_faq_090324.html and Federal Reserve Bank of New York, "FAQs: Purchasing Direct Obligations of Housing-Related GSEs," press release, April 21, 2009, http://www.newyorkfed.org/ markets/gses_faq_090421.html.

[6] Federal Housing Finance Agency, "Questions and Answers on Conservatorship," press release, September 7, 2008, http://www.treasury.gov/press/releases/reports/fhfa_consrv_ faq_090708hp1128.pdf.

[7] Mortgage-backed securities (MBS) are pools of mortgages that Fannie Mae and Freddie Mac combine and guarantee. The size and guarantee make MBS more attractive to institutional investors. Federal Housing Finance Agency, Current Data on Treasury and Federal Reserve Purchase Programs for GSE and Mortgage-Related Securities, August 20, 2009, http://www.fhfa.gov/webfiles/14778/TSYFed082009.pdf.

[8] P.L. 110-289, Sec. 1145. Actual dissolution of a GSE would require Congressional action.

[9] In addition, the GSEs purchase multifamily mortgages. These multifamily mortgages are a relatively small portion of the GSEs' purchases. In 2008, Fannie Mae purchased $617 billion of mortgages of which $34 billion were multifamily. In the same year, Freddie Mac purchased $382 billion of mortgages including $24 billion of multifamily mortgages. Source: Federal Housing Finance Agency, *2008 Report to Congress*, 2008, p. 122, http://www.fhfa.gov/webfiles/2335/FHFA_ReportToCongress2008508.pdf.

[10] Most 30-year mortgages are paid off because of refinancing or moving in 7 to 10 years. On average, the GSEs need to finance a 30-year mortgage (or MBS) held in portfolio for this 7 to 10 year time period.

[11] For more on conservatorship and receivership, see CRS Report RL34657, *Financial Institution Insolvency: Federal Authority over Fannie Mae, Freddie Mac, and Depository Institutions*, by David H. Carpenter and M. Maureen Murphy.

[12] CRS Report RS22963, *Financial Market Intervention*, by Edward V. Murphy and Baird Webel.

[13] On February 18, 2009, Treasury announced that it was increasing each GSE's portfolio limit from $850 billion to $900 billion. See U.S. Treasury, "Statement by Secretary Tim Geithner on Treasury's Commitment to Fannie Mae and Freddie Mac," press release, February 18, 2009, http://www.treasury.gov/press/releases/tg32.htm, U.S. Treasury, "Amended and Restated Senior Preferred Stock Purchase Agreement," press release, September 26, 2008, http://www.treasury.gov/press/releases/reports/seniorpreferredstockpurchaseagreementfnm1 .pdf, and U.S. Treasury, "Amended and Restated Senior Preferred Stock Purchase Agreement," press release, September 26, 2008, http://www.treasury.gov/press/releases/ reports/seniorpreferredstockpurchaseagreementfrea.pdf.

[14] CRS Report RL34423, *Government Interventions in Financial Markets: Economic and Historic Analysis of Subprime Mortgage Options*, by N. Eric Weiss, and CRS Report RS22956, *The Cost of Government Financial Interventions, Past and Present*, by Baird Webel, Marc Labonte, and N. Eric Weiss analyze selected past government actions. Information on Fannie Mae's and Freddie Mac's warrants is available at U.S. Treasury, "Federal National Mortgage Association: Warrant to Purchase Common Stock," press release, September 7, 2008, http://www.treasury.gov/press/releases/reports/warrantfnm3.pdf and U.S. Treasury, "Federal Home Loan Mortgage Corporation: Warrant to Purchase Common Stock," press release, September 7, 2008, http://www.treasury.gov/press/ releases/reports/warrantfrec.pdf. See also, CRS Report R40005, *Chrysler Corporation Loan Guarantee Act of 1979: Background, Provisions, and Cost*, by James M. Bickley.

[15] Fannie Mae became stockholder owned in 1968 by *Housing and Urban Development Act of 1968*, P.L. 90-448, 82 Stat. 536, and Freddie Mac in 1989 by *Financial Institutions Reform, Recovery, and Enforcement Act of 1989*, P.L. 101-73, 103 Stat. 429.

[16] Miscellaneous Revenue Act of 1982, P.L. 97-362, 96 Stat. 1726 et seq.

[17] Current GSE affordable housing goals were published in Federal Housing Finance Agency, "2009 Enterprise Transition Affordable," 74 *Federal Register* 20236-20263, May 1, 2009.

[18] FHFA currently has authority to approve new products, (HERA, Section 1123).

[19] Conforming mortgages are those that conform to Fannie Mae's and Freddie Mac's purchase standards including the conforming loan limit, downpayment, and credit history. The phrase "conforming loan" is sometimes used to mean all loans at or below the conforming loan limit, regardless of any other factors that might make them ineligible for GSE purchase. For more on the conforming loan limit, see CRS Report RS22172, *The Conforming Loan Limit*, by N. Eric Weiss and Mark Jickling.

[20] According to this reasoning, the precise number of GSEs is of little importance as long as there are enough GSEs to provide meaningful competition, and no one GSE is "too big to fail."

[21] Rosalind L. Bennett, Mark D. Vaughan, and Timothy J. Yeager, "Should the FDIC Worry About the FHLB? The Impact of Federal Home Loan Bank Advances on the Bank Insurance Fund," FDIC Center for Financial Research, Working Paper 2005-10, August 18, 2006, http://www.fdic.gov/bank/analytical/cfr/2005/wp2005/ CFRWP_2005_10_Bennett_ Vaughan_Yeager.pdf.

[22] Olaf de Senerpont Domis, "Sallie Mae Shifting Gears For Move to Private Sector Series: 10," *American Banker*, November 13, 1996, p. 4, and Jaret Seiberg, "House Data Have

Economists Gazing at a Murky Crystal Ball Series: 3," *American Banker*, September 26, 1996, p. 1.

[23] *Student Loan Marketing Association Reorganization Act of 1996*, P.L. 104-208.

[24] Andreas Lehnert, Wayne Passmore, and Shane Sherlund, *GSEs, Mortgage rates, and Secondary Market Activity*, Federal Reserve Board, 2006-30, Washington, DC, 2006, http://www.federalreserve.gov/pubs/feds/2006/200630/ 200630pap.pdf.

[25] Ibid.

[26] Mortgage Bankers' Association, *National Delinquency Survey*, Second Quarter 2009, pp. 4, 6.

[27] Inside Mortgage Finance Publications, *The 2009 Mortgage Market Statistical Annual*, vol. 2, p. 10.

[28] CRS Report RS22925, *Covered Bonds: An Alternative to Securitization for Funding Mortgages*, by Edward V. Murphy.

[29] U.S. Treasury, "Fact Sheet: Treasury Releases Best Practices For Residential Covered Bonds," press release, June 28, 2008, http://www.treas.gov/press/releases/reports/factsheet.pdf.

[30] Federal Deposit Insurance Corporation, "Covered Bond Policy Statement," 73 *Federal Register* 21951, April 23, 2008.

[31] Federal Housing Finance Agency, "U.S. Treasury Support for Fannie Mae and Freddie Mac," press release, January 18, 2009, http://www.fhfa.gov/webfiles/1240/ mmnote091_218091.pdf.

[32] U.S. Department of the Treasury, *Financial Regulatory Reform: A New Foundation*, August 11, 2009, pp. 41-42, http://www.financialstability.gov/docs/regs/FinalReport_web

CHAPTER SOURCES

Chapter 1 - This is an edited, reformatted and augmented version of a U.S. Department of Housing and Urban Development publication, dated February, 2011.

Chapter 2 - This is an edited, reformatted and augmented version of a Congressional Research Services publication, RL34661, dated December 20, 2010.

Chapter 3 - This is an edited, reformatted and augmented version of a Congressional Research Services publication, R40800, dated September 17, 2009.

INDEX

G

H

I

J

L

U

V

W